Detail of sponge graining on Farmington clock (Pl. 17). Collection of Kenneth and Paulette Tuttle, Randolph, Maine.

SIMPLE FORMS
AND VIVID COLORS

SIMPLE FORMS AND VIVID COLORS:

An Exhibition of Maine Painted Furniture, 1800-1850
at The Maine State Museum
July 8, 1983 - February 28, 1984

by

Edwin A. Churchill

Curator of Decorative Arts
Maine State Museum: Augusta

Foreword by Dean A. Fales, Jr.

Published by The MAINE STATE MUSEUM

— 1983 —

Front Cover:
Decorations kit found in Maine and in use ca. 1850-1900. M.S.M., 80.98.1.

Library of Congress Catalog Card Number 83-61807

International Standard Book Number 0-913764-15-9

Printed in United States of America by
The Knowlton & McLeary Co.

Table of Contents

Foreword

The quarter century between 1825 and 1850 has been called the Golden Age of American painted furniture. While the Powdered Bronze Age would be more accurate terminology, the fact remains that during this period a vast number of painted and decorated pieces of all descriptions were produced in rural and urban areas all around the country. Through a certain stylishness and economy — cheap chic in modern parlance — painted furniture was within the reach of everyone, and everyone reached for it.

This period coincided with Maine's emergence as a state, and a resulting spirit of thankful liberation can be imagined in some of the painted furniture made here. The decoration, though less flamboyant than that of Pennsylvania and New York State productions, usually has a reserved, northern air. On occasion, some really wild imaginative painting was splashed on a chest or a box. Maine decorated furniture, however, was generally quite sombre and derivative. It was made in quantities that helped much of it survive the raspy refinishers of a century later.

A number of painted pieces were brought to Maine from other cabinetmaking centers. In 1825, Daniel Wise & Co. advertised "BOSTON FURNITURE" in the *Kennebunk Gazette* (September 3). He mentioned that he kept constantly for sale "at Boston prices" looking glasses, "Brown, Yellow and Green Chairs with Gilt Backs" (from 4s 6d to 7s 6d each), work tables, elegant dressing tables, wash stands, and mahogany bureaus and card tables.

This exhibition brings together many documented examples of Maine painted furniture, as well as listings of decorators and makers. It demonstrates vividly the wide diversity of form and decoration that characterized the productions of the first half of the nineteenth century. The documented pieces are the pegs of certainty on which future attributions will be hung. There will be new discoveries always, but here, for the first time, the worthiness of a part of Maine's heritage can be seen, assessed, and above all enjoyed.

Dean A. Fales, Jr.
Kennebunkport, Maine

Acknowledgements

Several months ago I approached our Director, Paul Rivard, with what I now realize was a very energetic proposal for an exhibition and catalog on Maine painted furniture, to be ready for a July, 1983 opening. He asked one fundamental question: "Can it be done in the time available?"

That turned out to be an excellent question; and if it had not been for the assistance of numerous individuals, the deadline could not have been reached. Shortly after the project was under way, Karen Harvey, an intern from the University of Leicester, England, arrived at the Museum. She soon found herself involved with the exhibition catalog, preparing artifact descriptions and helping organize the decorators checklist. As the catalog neared completion, Karen ended up handling a wide variety of tasks, and proved a most effective and unconscionably cheerful assistant. Also helping with the catalog, Museum volunteer Louise Hathaway was instrumental in compiling and ordering data for the checklist.

As always, fellow staff members were most helpful. Stephen Brooke examined well over a hundred wood samples and along with Don Bassett prepared the furniture for photography and the upcoming exhibition. Jane Radcliffe and Marilyn Norcini helped edit and proofread the text. Marion Smith, Gertrude Drake and Arlene Moody suffered the doleful task of typing and retyping copies of the catalog and Greg Hart carried a large part of the burden of photographing the pieces. Besides helping edit the catalog and providing a number of suggestions along the way, Paul Rivard was instrumental in getting the catalog approved, funded and through the various phases of publication. It was finally up to Paul Plumer, project consultant, to get the catalog designed and coordinate the layout and printing. He did it with a flair.

It was a pleasure to have Kenneth Jewett and Stephen Weston prepare essays on stenciling and graining. Both are accomplished practitioners of their crafts and good writers as well. Their articles add a fine touch to the catalog. And a special thanks must go to Dean Fales, Jr., who was most helpful as I polished up the final manuscript.

Certainly one of the most important groups to be thanked are those who provided objects for the exhibition and inclusion in the catalog. The items they loaned are truly fine expressions of Maine painted furniture, and special appreciation is extended to Charles and Nancy Burden, Burton and Helaine Fendelman, Roberta Hansen, George Morrill, Earle G. Shettleworth, Jr., Kenneth Tuttle, Arlie Porath, the Farnsworth Museum of Art, the Metropolitan Museum of Fine Arts, and the Shelburne Museum, Inc.

Earle G. Shettleworth, Jr., the Director of the Maine Historic Preservation Commission, was also immensely helpful in locating information and providing leads to exhibitable objects. Only a phone call away, and a long-time scholar of Maine artifacts and architecture, he many times helped me with a specific question. There were many others who helped as well, including Nancy Goyne Evans, Laura Sprague, Thomas Gaffney, Samuel Pennington, Charles and Betty Berdan, Lester Dumond, Robert Foster, Jr., David Jewell, James Julia, Ross Levett, Bill and Arlene Schwind, Joy Piscopo, Peggy Grant, David Morse, and Mrs. Hugh Mosher.

Still, no matter how much assistance one receives, the proclivity and certainty of errors is beyond doubt. Unfortunately, those which do appear in the publication are one of the few things I must claim wholly of my own making.

Edwin A. Churchill

Abbreviations

AA - *American Advocate* (Hallowell)
AC - *Augusta Courier*
b. - born
bass - basswood
BD - *Bangor Directory*
BDWC - *Bangor Daily Whig and Courier*
BG - *Belfast Gazette*
BR - *Bangor Register*
BRPA - *Bangor Register and Penobscot Advertiser*
CCRD - Cumberland County Registry of Deeds
CIEC - *Christian Intelligencer and Eastern Chronicle* (Gardiner)
d. - died
D. - overall depth of object
EA - *Eastern Argus* (Portland)
Ells Am - *Ellsworth American*
FC, 1850: Me., r., p. - Federal Census, 1850: Maine, microfilm roll, page
FIC, 1850: Me., p., no. - Federal Industrial Census, 1850: Maine, page, number
H. - overall height of object
HG - *Hallowell Gazette*
HGPP - *Hancock Gazette and Penobscot Patriot* (Belfast)
ISMR - *Independent Statesman and Maine Republican* (Portland)
J - *Jeffersonian* (Portland)
KCRD - Kennebec County Registry of Deeds

KCRP - Kennebec County Registry of Probate
KJ - *Kennebec Journal*
LFJ - *Lewiston Falls Journal*
LRG - *Limerock Gazette* (E. Thomaston)
MBD - *Maine Business Directory*
MELCA - *Maine Enquirer and Lincoln County Advertiser* (Bath)
MF - *Maine Farmer* (Winthrop)
MG - *Maine Gazette* (Bath)
MI - *Maine Inquirer* (Bath)
MP - *Maine Palladium* (Saco)
MPSG - *Maine Patriot and State Gazette* (Augusta)
MSM - Maine State Museum
OD - *Oxford Democrat* (Paris)
OT - *Oriental Trumpet* (Portland)
PA - *Portland Advertiser*
PD - *Portland Directory*
PG - *Portland Gazette*
PJ - *Penobscot Journal* (Bangor)
PT - *Portland Transcript*
RJ - *Republican Journal* (Bangor)
TR - *The Radical* (Ellsworth)
USD - *United States Democrat* (Rockland)
W. - overall width of object
w. - worked
W/P - white pine

Explanations

Dimensions: The measurements of (H.) height, (W.) width and (D.) depth are the overall dimensions, taken from the extreme points of each piece. An exception to this format is the Stewart Windsor chair (No. 1) whose dimensions are listed as (H.) height, (SW.) seat width and (SD.) seat depth; the format used in Charles Santore's *The Windsor Style in America* which features the chair.

Citations: A source is listed in full when it appears initially in the text. In all other instances, the same source is shortlisted.

Arrangement: The furniture pieces are arranged in the catalog section according to type; such as chair, stand, box, etc.

Ownership: The majority of the pieces featured in the catalog are part of the Maine State Museum's collection. These pieces are credited with the Museum's abbreviation, MSM, and their accession number, such as 75.61.3. In those cases where the Museum has acquired a piece through donation, it is so stated. All other pieces are on loan to the Museum for the duration of the exhibition and are credited to the individual or institutional owners.

Maine Towns: Maine did not attain statehood until 1820. However, for the purpose of simplification, present-day Maine towns which are mentioned in the text in connection with dates prior to 1820 remain listed as Maine towns, rather than Massachusetts.

Introduction

There is something special about the brightly painted furniture that enlivened Maine homes in the first half of the nineteenth century. Bold, graphic, and seemingly naive, these pieces reflect a simpler, less cluttered time, a folk culture yet untamed by the strictures of the modern world. Or do they?

Such a view is immediately disturbed by the vast variations in the spirit of presentation. The *trompe l'oeil* rosewood graining on a New Sharon melodeon forces a second and searching look before it reveals its true nature. The carefully ordered striping and stencil work on a yellow Portland chair projects a need for sophistication and control. Then, at the other extreme, rests a small box from the upper Kennebec Valley. Red/black graining swirls and loops across the surfaces, and appears so lightly attached that it seems ready to leap from its pine backing were it not held down by a unique group of dramatic and exotic stencils. If the painter of this box shines forth as an identifiable artist, brimming with zeal and creativity, there were far more who clearly copied the work of others — previous and contemporary — creating several large bodies of typical Maine patterns. The more deeply we look, the more complex that long-lost world, the less naive the inhabitants. Decoration served many functions, and the decorators represented a body of craftsmen with widely divergent styles and abilities. It is a world worthy of more careful scrutiny.

Unpainted dressing table made by J.P. Caffrey, Waterville, Maine. Anonymous loan. The decorated companion was constructed by Madison Tuck of Hallowell, Maine (Pl. 4). Donated by Maine Antiques Digest, Waldoboro, Maine.

Section I.

Simple Forms and Vivid Colors

If there is a single motivation which would best explain the popularity of painted Maine furniture during the first half of the nineteenth century, it would have to be the desire for elegance and beauty without much money to pay for it. Decorated furniture was the vernacular answer to rich rosewood and gleaming mahogany pieces that graced the homes of Maine's more affluent. In deference, some pieces carefully mimicked the wood grain and decoration of their more stately counterparts; others exalted in the decorative opportunities afforded by paint, and revealed lively inspirations derived from their own surroundings and folk culture.

Woods and Construction

Builders of furniture destined for decoration had one major goal — to keep the cost down — and one way to do that was to purchase inexpensive materials. The wood they used was locally harvested, of common varieties, and often of less than the best quality. Microanalysis of specific elements on thirty-nine different pieces of Maine furniture was carried out by Museum conservator Stephen Brooke between December 1, 1982, and February 10, 1983 (see Appendix A). A review of the findings revealed a number of patterns, some which seem quite reasonable, others which were a bit surprising.

An inspection of four case pieces (i.e., a bureau, a desk, and two two-drawer blanket chests) indicated some specific tendencies. Primary woods (including tops, cases, and drawer fronts) were all of white pine, except for birch drawer fronts on one blanket chest and a birch drawer divider between the top and second drawer of the desk. Drawer interiors on these pieces were of basswood except for the desk which used white pine. Turned legs were of either birch or beech.

Stands and tables (i.e., three dressing tables, two wash stands and one plain stand) had a somewhat different pattern. Frames and drawer fronts were largely of white pine. A major exception was one dressing table constructed solely of basswood except for a single upper case drawer made of pine. A second was a washstand of which the lower half of the case was pine and the upper of basswood. Drawer interiors were of basswood with two exceptions. Surprisingly, the tops and the legs of these stands and tables also tend to be of basswood, with only two white pine tops and one set of white pine legs.

Similarly, basswood proved a great favorite for boxes. Of seven boxes examined, five were constructed of basswood, one was built from pine and one was made of a less common local soft hardwood, tupelo.

Chairs offered a bit more diversity than other forms, but certainly not as much as often is claimed in publications on the topic. There were generally a limited number of wood types utilized, with basswood and pine for plank seats, and beech, birch and maple for other elements. In the analysis of sixteen different chairs, it was possible to segregate and compare three plank seat chairs made by Samuel White of Fairfield, Dexter, Exeter, etc., and four similar items made by the Walter Corey Company of Portland. White proved to be a model of consistency. Every chair tested had a basswood seat and was otherwise of birch. The only non-birch elements on any were maple armrests and rockers on a Salem rocking chair. Corey's operation illustrated a different pattern. The seats on his chairs were all basswood, and for other elements he used birch, beech or maple. However, he treated the woods as interchangeable and on those four pieces were found back posts of three different types of woods, and most other elements could be found in at least two varieties.

Looking to those chairs not made by White or Corey, one finds great diversity of usage within a narrow variety of woods. Back posts were made of beech, maple, and birch; legs were of beech and maple; and spindles and stretchers were of poplar (aspen) and birch. Also, some seats were of white pine as well as basswood.

3

CHART I: Casepieces, Tables and Stands (Main Woods)

Casepieces	Case	Top	Drawer Fronts	Drawer Interior	Back Boards	Legs
Merrill Empire Bureau (Plate 12)	White pine (W/P)	W/P	W/P	Basswood (Bass)	W/P	Beech
Alexander Empire Desk (Plate 15)	W/P	W/P	W/P	W/P	W/P	Beech
New Portland Blanket Chest (Plate 9)	W/P	W/P	Birch	Bass	W/P	
Tobey Blanket Chest (Plate 10)	W/P		W/P	Bass	W/P	Birch

Tables/Stands	Frame	Top	Drawer Fronts	Drawer Interior	Back Boards	Legs
Tobey Washstand (Plate 7)	W/P	Bass	W/P	Bass	W/P	Bass
Tobey Dressing Table (Plate 7)	W/P	Bass	W/P	Bass		Bass
Readfield Dressing Table (Plate 5)	Bass	Bass	W/P (sm. dr.) Bass (lg. dr.)	W/P (sm. dr.) Bass (lg. dr.)		Bass
Carney Stand (Plate 3)	W/P	W/P	W/P	W/P		W/P
Tuck Dressing Table (Plate 4)	W/P	W/P	W/P	Bass		Bass
Hubbard Washstand (Plate 8)	W/P (lower) Bass (upper)	Bass (lower) Bass (upper)	W/P	Bass		Bass

CHART II: Chairs (Main Woods)

Cane Seat Chairs	Seat	Back Posts	Crest Rail	Spindles	Legs	Stretchers	Misc.
Corey Hitchcock Side Chair (Plate 26)	Maple	Birch			Birch		
Corey Fancy Side Chair (Plate 27)	Maple	Beech			Beech		
Todd & Beckett Fancy Side Chair (Plate 27)	Birch				Birch		
Corey Windsor/Hitchcock							
Side Chair (loan - anon)	Bass	Beech	Birch	Birch	Birch	Birch	
Side Chair (MSM 73.93.4)	Bass	Maple			Beech	Beech	
Side Chair (loan - Shettleworth)	Bass				Beech	Beech	
Side Chair (Plate 26)	Bass	Beech			Beech	Birch	
White Chairs							
Thumb-Back Side Chair (Fairfield) (MSM 80.139.1)	Bass				Birch	Birch	
Thumb-Back Side Chair (Exeter) (MSM 78.12.1)	Bass	Birch	Birch	Birch	Birch	Birch	
Salem Rocker (Exeter) (Plate 30)	Bass	Birch	Birch				Maple armrest + rocker
Misc. Plank Seat							
Tobey Boston Rocker (Plate 31)	Bass	Beech			Beech		Birch armpost Beech rocker
Set of four Thumb-Back Side Chairs (Plate 24)	W/P	Maple		Poplar (Aspen)	Beech	Birch	
"JCT" Fancy Side Chair (Plate 25)	softwood	Birch	Maple		Maple		
Capen Arrow-Back Side Chair (Fig. 9)	W/P	Maple or Birch			Maple		
Slat Backs							
Side Chair (Plate 28)	Beech				Birch		
Child's Arm Chair (Plate 28)	Ash	Maple	Ash (slats)		Maple		

In retrospect, the makers were using a limited number of local wood varieties and they usually used the woods where they were most effective. Soft, carvable white pine and basswood made fine seats and light, durable drawer interiors. Birch, beech and maple were found on turned elements and where they might be needed for added strength. Of course, makers were not adverse to a bit of corner cutting. Consequently, one finds basswood legs and poplar spindles, woods by no means best for the job — on the other hand, they were cheap and easily worked.

The major wood varieties identified by microanalysis are echoed in the advertisements and account books of Maine cabinetmakers and chairmakers. Samuel Smith and Moses Wells of Augusta, John Brown of Hallowell, and Samuel Sinkler and Loring Varney of Belfast were all advertising for birch boards and joists. Smith was also looking for maple boards.[1] Several makers were seeking pine and basswood; John Brown, J.B. Pierce of Augusta, and Amaziah Moore and Horatio Beale of Bangor were especially so — needing these easily carvable woods for chair seats.[2] The needs of at least two local makers are delineated in an 1827 advertisement by Saco craftsmen Adams and Libby. They were looking for the following:

10,000 feet of birch and maple joist, 3 by 4 inches
2,000 feet of birch joist, 4 by 4 inches, 1 quality
2,000 feet of birdseye maple joist, 4 by 4 inches
2,000 feet of birch boards
1,000 feet of poplar plank, 2 and 2½ inches
2,000 feet of poplar and bass joist, 3 by 4 inches.[3]

The daybooks of three Maine cabinetmakers corroborate the data from other sources. Nathaniel Knowlton of Eliot reported using pine, basswood, birch, maple, and ash; David Knowlton of Augusta used the same woods plus mahogany; and John Brewer of Brewer recorded pine, birch, and maple.[4]

The reason for the woods selected for decorated furniture is simple — price. The account books of the two Knowltons and Brewer reveal specific cost structures. Hardwoods and pine all cost approximately the same. What is eminently clear, though, is that these local woods were several times cheaper than their prestigious counterpart, mahogany.

Costs of Wood (1815-1836) [cents-per-foot]

Pine	.8 - 3. cents
Basswood	.67 - 3. cents
Birch	1. - 2. cents
Maple	1.5 - 3. cents
Ash	1.5
Mahogany	12.5 - 75. cents

Obviously these figures mask a variety of more complex details. For example, on October 21, 1835, John Brewer listed number 2 pine at 1.8¢ per foot, and number 3 at 1.2¢. On October 12, a year later, he listed

number 1 lumber (probably pine) at 2.5¢ per foot, number 2 at 2.3¢; number 3 at 1.2¢; and number 4 at .8¢.[5] Interestingly, on that date, he bought 319 feet of numbers 1 and 2 lumber, and 1,314 feet of numbers 3 and 4. In all probability, some of the lower-grade lumber that Brewer purchased ended up in his less expensive furniture, including sinks, cradles, chests, a washstand, and a desk for a schoolhouse.[6]

That this would not have been a singular case is suggested by the poor quality of wood frequently found on decorated pieces. For example, the right side of a small stand found in Sheepscot (Plate 3) has a painted-over knot along the upper edge. A knot can also be seen in the rear leg of a stand made by William A. Mason of Fryeburg, Maine (Fig. 7). And a dressing table constructed by Madison Tuck of Hallowell (Plate 4) has even worse materials; but they, at least, are interior elements.

Decorated furniture tends to be simply, and sometimes poorly, constructed. On case pieces, the backboards are rabbeted and nailed into the sides; unlike better items, they are never mortised into back corner posts. On two pieces, a blanket chest from the Solon area (Plate 11) and one from the Tobey estate in Fairfield (Plate 10), the makers didn't even bother to fully rabbet in the backboards. Thus, strips of end grain run along the back edges of the sides, concealed only by paint.

Moldings and carved elements rarely grace decorated furniture of the first half of the nineteenth century. An exception is a cupboard (or buffet) from Madawaska, Maine (Plate 16), a survival piece reflecting earlier bold French traditions. The cornice, midsection, and the bracket base all have well-shaped molded surfaces which serve to complement the raised panels and to spatially organize the large mass of the piece. In its powerful, joined form, the cupboard is more an exception to, rather than an example of, mainstream Maine decorated furniture.

The simplicity of construction also appears in the turned elements of the furniture. On a few pieces, such as a desk from the Jonas Alexander estate in Hiram (Plate 15) sharp, deep turnings provide an effective contrast to the flat, large surfaces of the mahogany drawer fronts. More typical is the Tuck table, (Plate 4), whose ring turnings and ring and ball feet seem weak in comparison.

Vernacular furniture exhibited increasing simplification as mid-century approached, largely because of changing manufacturing patterns exhibited by the growing number of furniture factories found in the state. Utilizing anywhere from five to one hundred employees, these operations were steadily more dependent on standardized parts, use of machinery, and semiskilled labor. Such skilled tasks as bending, carving, and curved cutting were minimized and, where necessary, directed to a specialist in the firm. Both features are evident in the products of the Walter

Corey plant. A typical wood-seat chair (Plate 26) had a simply-curved seat, unbent turned elements (including spindles), and shallow ring turnings. An 1850 description of the Corey operation reflects the specialization of the plant, with separate machine-filled areas for rough cutting, seat shaping, and turning and boring, along with other sections for carving, assembly, and painting.[7] Similar organizational patterns are suggested in an 1843 article on the A. & E. Dole Company in Bangor.[8]

Unfortunately, simplicity is quite often matched with less than stellar craftsmanship. This is certainly true regarding dovetailing on box and drawer corners. Although some dovetails are really quite well done, there are more than a few that are imperfectly cut, poorly fitted, or simply rather coarse. The drawer dovetailings on the Alexander desk (Plate 15, and Fig. 1) are excessively wide, too short, set into too-deeply-cut mortises, and have thoroughly crooked edges. Not surprisingly, the fit is less than ideal.

Figure 1:   Alexander desk. MSM collection.

The artisans' shortcomings are visible in two items from the Tobey estate. A rocking settee (Plate 32) has sixteen spindles in the back measuring thirteen inches each, with a ball turning about a third of the way up the spindle. In theory, the balls should form a straight line across the back. In fact, almost no two are of the same height, and there is nearly a three-quarter of an inch difference between the highest and the lowest. A washstand (Plate 7) displays another example of mediocre craftsmanship. The legs were turned out of squared stock. The pieces available were slightly smaller than the pattern being used, thus at the widest part of each turned leg there are flat surfaces. Rather than rejecting such pieces, they were simply fastened to the stand, brightly painted and sent on their way.

It is no surprise that the materials, the construction methods, and the final finish made a great difference in the cost of a piece. This is explicitly demonstrated in the selling price of bureaus. In 1832, Moses Wells of Augusta was advertising bureaus priced from $6 to $28; in 1844, J. Simonds of Waterville was charging from $5 to $30; and, four years later, George Smith of Lewiston was asking $5.50 to $25.[9]

The account books of the specific makers provide some clues as to the relationship between quality and cost. From 1826 to 1828, David Knowlton of Augusta sold mahogany bureaus for $18 to $28, and mahogany front bureaus from $12 to $16. Birch counterparts sold from $7.25 to $14, and a pine piece went for $5. These last two categories — plus chests,[10] which sold from $2.50 to $3.00 — were the most frequent recipients of a coat of paint. Nathaniel Knowlton of Eliot and an anonymous maker from Bath[11] documented similar trends in their daybooks.

Nathaniel Knowlton made a number of references to the production of painted furniture. On June 4, 1824, he noted selling a "chest painted" for $2.50, and on October 17, 1827, he charged a customer $2.25 for "making a chest, formed [?] lock and hinges and painting." On April 14, the same year, he sold what must have been a rather special item: "a birch bureau [with] turned pillars [and] with backboard ornamented." That cost $12 — a fairly good sum for a piece of decorated furniture.

The Decoration

Painted furniture features two very different although not always separate approaches. The first provides an all-over surface treatment through graining, and the second offers a wide variety of specific decorative elements and motifs through free-hand painting, stenciling, striping, and an assortment of lesser techniques.

Graining gained favor in America in the early eighteenth century. In most instances it was generally stylized, suggesting rather than representing specific woods. The practice declined in popularity in the late eighteenth century, but had a rebirth in the early 1800s. This time the graining tended to be more realistic,[1] and it received widespread acceptance among the middle and lower classes as an alternative to the prohibitively expensive fine woods used on furniture of the more affluent. It flourished in rural regions where makers frequently worked in conservative forms and patterns but in simplified, less subtle, and at times, startling and bold ways. Local proclivities, folk traditions, and individual creativity gave an unexpected richness to many of the grained pieces emerging from the rural milieu.

Mahogany was one of the most frequently copied grains. The earliest documented Maine piece is a Hepplewhite bureau constructed by E. Morse of Livermore in 1814 (Fig. 2). The red-on-yellow graining

Figure 2: Morse bureau. Photograph courtesy of the Henry Ford Museum, The Edison Institute.

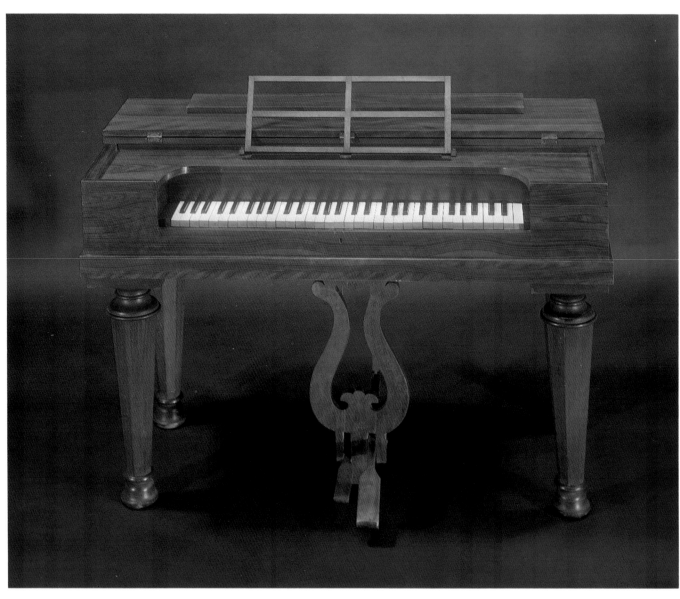

Figure 3:   Chase melodeon. MSM collection.

closely resembles mahogany, and the drawer edges have been given deceptively convincing painted dentil borders.[2] Such graining remained popular well into the nineteenth century, and was used on a small box made for Esther Leighton of Augusta, Maine in 1847 (Plate 5). Grained to simulate figured wood, the piece is wholly typical except for a strange green oval reserve in the center of the top.

Rosewood was another commonly imitated variety. A wood popularized in the Empire period,[3] the graining often appeared on pieces reflecting Empire characteristics. Numerous vase-back, often Klismos-style, chairs from the Walter Corey Company in Portland were rosewood grained (Plate 27); likewise, those made by contemporaneous townsmen William Todd and Samuel S. Beckett were similarly decorated (Plate 27). Not surprisingly, a melodeon constructed by G. W. Chase of New Sharon (Fig. 3) was carefully grained to simulate rosewood. Considering the popularity of this wood on keyboard pieces of the period, Chase was clearly looking to the finer examples in his effort to dress up the plain hardwood case.

Bird's-eye maple was a third wood frequently mimicked by Maine decorators, often on specific furniture elements such as drawer fronts and chair seats. A Boston rocker from the Tobey estate in Fairfield is representative (Plate 31). Red-and-black grained with yellow trim, its presence is greatly enhanced by the inclusion of a simulated bird's-eye maple seat.

Then there is a dressing table that can be traced to the Readfield region as early as the 1830s (Plate 5). Both the maker and decorator (if not the same person) were quite individualistic. The piece is perched on extraordinarily long and well-turned legs, and has a backboard with exuberant lines. The decoration is equally striking. The drawer fronts are grained to simulate mahogany, the ends and legs are painted as bird's-eye maple, and the top and backboard have yet a third, possibly plain maple, graining. The piece is exceptional in another way, for someone covered the bottom of the upper case and upper case drawer with political slogans. A strong National Republican and supporter of Henry Clay, the author wrote ''Clay Forever'' and ''Clayites in Readfield.'' He praised National Republicans Jonathan Hunton of Readfield and Daniel Goodnow of Alfred. The first served as Maine Governor for the period 1829-30, and the second unsuccessfully tried for the post in 1831, 1832, and 1833.[4] Andrew Jackson, a Democrat, received less favorable remarks. Our sloganist referred to him as a ''Jackas'' and then went on to note that there were ''Few Jackson Jackasses'' in Readfield.

Not all grained pieces were realistically done. Harking back to eighteenth-century traditions, many showed stylized and simplified patterns, suggestive at best of specific grains. The looping red-on-black graining on a chest from South Paris only tentatively suggests crotch mahogany veneers (Plate 12), and the striped black-on-red decoration on a matching washstand and dressing table from the Fairfield Tobey estate seems even less like the rosewood grain that was the inspiration (Plate 7). Also, the graining on a small box from Rumford was probably derived from rosewood examples (Plate 21), but the exotic application, including large yellow pointed ovoids (heartwood?), is stylized almost beyond recognition.

Some patterns were developed that seem purely decorative and non-imitative. Numerous Maine pieces were sponge-grained, a process creating a rippled effect often applied in patterned motifs. A tall clock found in the Farmington area and housing the works of Winchester, Connecticut, clockmaker Riley Whiting, is a striking specimen (Plate 17). The piece has sponged orange-and-cream graining with red and yellow daubed accents. The grain has been formed into a spiral pattern on the base and sides, adding significantly to the overall impact. This example is similar to a substantial number of decorated tall case clocks with mid-Maine provenances, in that the makers of the works were out-of-state.

Among other examples are two grained tall clocks found in the Waterville and Belgrade areas respectively, and both containing works manufactured by Silas Hoadley of Plymouth, Connecticut. Interestingly, the Belgrade piece bore the mark ''Bushed [?] and repaired by Arthur W. Spaulding, Feb. 20, 1869.'' This was probably Arthur Spaulding of Norridgewock, or possibly his son Arthur William Spaulding.[5]

The reason for this phenomenon is pretty much straightforward. By the second quarter of the nineteenth century, major clockmakers from Massachusetts and Connecticut were shipping out large quantities of works. Many were brought to Maine and fitted into locally made cases. For example, two cabinetmakers producing cases for imported works were Daniel Howard and Thomas T. Brown of Belfast, Maine. Both had substantial careers as cabinetmakers. In 1845 they joined in a partnership and for the next few years were ''manufacturing'' clocks. Those still extant have locally made rectangular ogee cases and contain purchased works.[6]

Less dramatic than the Farmington clock, and thereby more typical, is a salmon-colored, sponge-grained box from the Weston family homestead in Madison, Maine (Plate 21). Dark blue feathery decorations on the corners and the top edge add an extra touch. Without that, the piece would have been quite ordinary.

Smoke graining was another technique to appear frequently on Maine pieces.[7] Perhaps a vestigial survival of marbled graining, it had developed as an identifiable form early in the nineteenth century. As with simulated bird's-eye maple, smoke decoration was often applied to furniture elements rather than to the whole piece. The small yellow stand, found in

Sheepscot (Plate 3), is fairly typical with its smoke-grained top. A more dramatic example is a decorated Empire bureau found at Rumford Point (Plate 13). The yellow case, black-painted vase-turned legs, red striping, and green banding are already striking. The smoke-decorated drawer fronts move the piece into a class of its own.

As with graining, the story of nineteenth-century painted and stenciled decorative elements began over a century earlier. It can be traced back to the introduction of japanning, a technique developed to copy oriental lacquered furniture. The process was in vogue in England by the late 1600s, and was introduced to American by the early eighteenth-century. Japanning had some popularity in the colonies until about the mid-eighteenth century, when it declined in fashion. The previously-raised vignettes were increasingly done in flat gilt and, although Chinese scenes and figures were still popular, European (especially classical) motifs appeared more frequently. By the late 1700s, few American decorators used japanning to embellish their furniture; however, as the Federal period emerged, many ornamentors applied the numerous motifs in a far more straightforward process — decorative painting. Both George Hepplewhite and Thomas Sheraton promoted painted decoration on furniture. Having eschewed the richly carved curvilinear forms of the Chippendale era, they popularized clean, uncluttered lines derived from classical inspirations, and looked to veneers, inlays, and painted motifs to ornament their furniture.[9] The vignettes most often featured included various classical motifs as well as numerous naturalistic forms, including swags, wreaths, shells, and baskets or vases of fruit.[10]

Both men also addressed the topic of painting directly. Along with a number of general remarks in his *Cabinet-Maker and Upholsterer's Guide* (1794), Hepplewhite explicitly promoted the decoration of chairs.

> For chairs, a new and very elegant fashion has arisen within these few years, of finishing them with painted or japanned work, which gives a rich and splendid appearance to the minuter parts of the ornaments, which are generally thrown in by the painter. Several of these designs are particularly adapted to this style, which allows a framework less massy than is requisite for mahogany; and by assorting the prevailing colour to the furniture and light of the room affords opportunity, by the variety of grounds which may be introduced, to make the whole accord in harmony, with a pleasing and striking effect to the eye. Japanned chairs should have cane bottoms, with linen or cotton cases over cushions to accord with the general hue of the chair.[11]

Sheraton also suggested painting numerous elements

of the furniture illustrated in his *Cabinet-Maker and Upholsterer's Drawing Book* (1802), and he included a separate and detailed section on painting in his *Cabinet Dictionary* (1803).[12]

The contemporary impact of these two men is mirrored in one of the finest and earliest pieces of Maine decorated furniture, a mahogany and pine high-post bedstead made by Benjamin Radford of Portland in 1808. Constructed for townsman Stephen Longfellow, the bed cost twenty dollars plus an extra five dollars to decorate the pine cornice (Fig. 4). Painted orange, it has a black stripe along the bottom and a molding with a row of red circles at the top. At the center of both the sides and the end are trapezoidal tablets in which have been painted sprigs of oak leaves and acorns.[13]

Figure 4: Radford bed cornice. Courtesy of the Maine Historical Society.

Orange, rather than the then-popular white, the cornice might have been executed directly from the instruction in Sheraton's *Dictionary* regarding the ornamentation ''with leaves and some kind of trophey or flowers'' on bed and window cornices.

> As these do not require a great quantity of size, I advise only to give one lay of common whiting and size... when the surface of [the]...cornice is smooth and straight, one of size, and the rest in white lead and varnish..., give it a coat of clear varnish before the ornament is painted upon the ground. If their be any tablet in the centre, let this be painted last, that it may not be injured whilst the other parts are finishing. The ornaments should be sketched in with a black lead pencil, very light, and so as not to exceed the outline of the colour. And as the leaves and flowers are proceeded with, they should be nearly finished at the first painting.... When the work is finished thus far, to give it effect, it should be touched with highlights, and some strong shadows laid quick on... to give the greater force, as these things are viewed at a distance. Thus completed, give the work at least two coats of white hard varnish.[14]

Contemporaneous with the Radford bed was the development of female academies. Founded for the purpose of training young ladies in the skills of the polished gentlewoman, the course work provided basic academics, needlework, and art instruction which included drawing and painting.[15] A typical course fare is listed in the 1820 advertisement of Miss Aldrick, preceptress at the Cony Female Academy in Augusta. Her terms were:

> For Reading, Writing, Arithmetic, English Grammar, Rhetoric, Ancient and Modern Geography with the Use of the Globes and Maps, History, & c. with plain and Ornamental Needle Work, Print Work, Drawing and coloring Maps, & c. - - - $4 per Qr. Drawing, Painting in oil and water colors, Embroidery, including the above branches, - - - $7 per Qr.[16]

Although much of the drawing and painting done in these institutions would have been executed on paper or velvet, in New England more than a few young ladies tried their hands at decorating furniture, especially small tables and stands. A number of documented decorated tables probably came from one Maine school, the Bath Female Academy.[17] Three of these pieces are well-known classics in American decorated furniture. All are chamber tables with painted motifs applied on unpainted wood and two, done by Rachel and Elizabeth Paine Lombard in 1816 (see Plate 1 and Fig. 5), are extraordinarily similar. Essentially identical in form, they also feature closely related motifs. Both have vining leaves spiraling the legs and foliate sprays bordering the top edge. Squared reserves on the ends contain scenic views, and the tables feature elaborate foliate vines sinuously scrolling across the drawer fronts. Both have extensive literary material carefully written on their tops, including an ode to Bunker Hill on the Rachel Lombard piece and a poem entitled "Hope" on its companion. Only in the large top motifs do the tables differ significantly. Rachel used a view of "Limeric Castle," surrounded by birds and foliage. Elizabeth painted a large group of foliage and fruit similar to those found on theorem paintings of the period.[18]

Figure 5: Rachel H. Lombard table. Photograph courtesy of the Henry Francis du Pont Winterthur Museum.

The third table (see Fig. 6), decorated in 1815, is not as finely crafted as the other two; however, the ornamentation is equally interesting. A large landscape adorns the top, and painted views accent the ends. Delicate floral borders outline the top and drawer frame, and a banner undulates across the drawer front arching over a centered musical montage and bearing the inscription "Executed by Wealthy P. S. Jones, Bath, March 6, 1815." Vining flowers and foliage spread out and up from the center of the drawer, and fringe and tassel ornamentation accent the legs.[19] The overall effect is one of balance, color and sophistication.

The spirit of the Bath Academy pieces was still to be found a decade and a half later in a matching washstand and dressing table, the former signed by William A. Mason of Fryeburg, Maine, and dated August 24, 1829 (Figs. 7 & 8). The two pieces were painted white with green striping, had multicolored fruit and foliage groupings across the drawers, roses and foliage on the backboards, and scenes of ruins in landscapes on side panels. Yet they clearly differed from the Bath tables. Both were of simplified country Hepplewhite form, they were fully painted, their decorative motifs were more formalized in grouping and execution than those of their predecessors, and the scenic vignettes were very much of the Empire tradition. Unfortunately, the pair no longer exists, having been destroyed by fire in 1966.[20]

If the Mason pieces pointed to the vernacular expression of the Academy mentality, a delightful little stand found in Kents Hill, Maine portrays a folk-art interpretation (Plate 2). In many ways, the little stand is truer to academy art tradition. The decoration has been done on unpainted wood, delicate vining

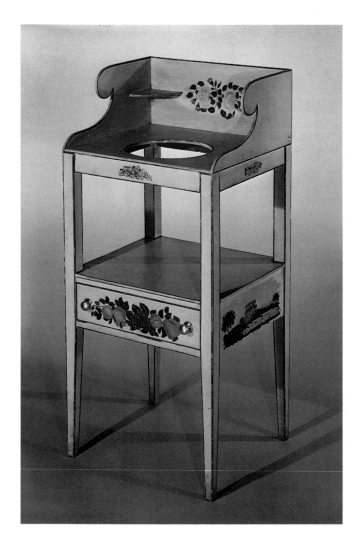

Figure 7: Mason washstand. Photograph courtesy of the Henry Ford Museum, The Edison Institute.

Figure 6: Wealthy P.S. Jones table. Photograph courtesy of the Henry Francis du Pont Winterthur Museum.

Figure 8: Mason dressing table. Photograph courtesy of the
Henry Ford Museum, The Edison Institute.

spirals up the legs and outlines major features, poems grace the drawer front and case back, and there is a major motif on the top and views on the side.

However, the decorations exude simplification, stylization, and naivete not present in the Bath tables. The exuberantly painted bowl of fruit depends on bold, colorful and simple patterns. It was clearly not executed by a professionally trained hand, a characteristic even more striking in the scenic vignettes on the sides of the stand. Rural views setting lightly on rolling green grounds feature simply painted houses and stylized trees. Perspective and shading are essentially missing. Charming in their simplicity, the scenes seem much in the spirit of the contemporaneous wall murals being painted by members of the Rufus Porter school. Even more intriguing is the fact that Porter and associate, Jonathan Poor, worked in the region in which this stand was found.[21]

The evolution of decorative styles so evident in the academy tables was similarly occurring in the ornamentation of furniture of the general populace. Probably the strongest vehicle for the evolution of ornamental motifs was decorated fancy furniture, especially the fancy chair. Many of the elements came straight out of Federal precedents. Yet, as the nineteenth century moved into the second and third decades, elements popular in the Empire period, such as pineapples and melons, began to appear on chair crest rails and back splats, and on other furniture forms.[22]

The popularity of the fancy chair in Maine is dramatically illustrated in the advertisements of local newspapers across the State. One of the earliest mentions was an 1803 notice by Nathaniel Frost of Portland that he was selling "Warranted Fancy, Bamboo, and Windsor Chairs and Settees."[23] Thirty years later, advertisements for fancy chairs could be found across the State. Michael Hogan of Bath was selling "Cane seat Fancy" chairs; Henry Noyes of Belfast had "Grecian Pattern Cane seat [chairs], common do, [i.e., ditto], flag seat do., and all kinds of fancy do., wooden seats"; John Brown of Hallowell was marketing "Cane and Flag bottom Fancy Chairs"; and Gardiner Brooks of Bangor could supply a large assortment of fancy and common chairs.[24]

The earliest group of documented Maine fancy chairs dates from c. 1815 to c. 1835, and sits squarely in the middle of major shifts in decorative techniques and patterns during the first half of the nineteenth century. Woods were frequently given a yellow coat of paint rather than the earlier white. The decorative motifs, while largely Federal in the 1810s, increasingly reflect Empire fashions with the passage of time. Free-hand painting was more frequently replaced by stencils, and the decoration gradually became more simplified and stylized.

An arrow-back Windsor rocking armchair made by John Brooks of Portland and decorated by partner John Hudson (Plate 29) is a fairly representative piece. The chair has squarish lines, a feature fairly common on contemporary chairs from southwestern Maine. Yellow painted, its back and comb crest rails are decorated with classic gold and green leaf scrolls. As is common with decorated furniture of the period, the chair has striped and banded ornamentation. Black stripes accentuate the seat and the bamboo-turned legs and stretchers, and light red/brown bands border the rails. As with the classical motifs, striping and banding were direct descendants of Federal decorative patterns, mimicking the string inlay so prevalent on furniture of that era.[25] Also, once again, one can look at Sheraton as a popularizer of the concept; in fact, at one point in his essay on paint, he stated that "black chairs look well when ornamented with yellow lines."[26] As our nineteenth century decorators were to demonstrate repeatedly, yellow lines also worked well on mahogany and rosewood graining.

A slightly later yellow-painted arrow-back side chair was built by William Capen, also of Portland (see Fig. 9). Similarly squarish, it has an oval seat, a bent back, and a shaped tableted center crest rail. Unfortunately, because of major paint retouching, the original design can only be generally described. The crest rail tablet contained a fruit and foliage grouping with centered plums (?), flanked by bunches of grapes and accented by cherries. Green leaves provided a background for the fruit. Very much like patterns seen on late fancy chairs and other period furniture, the formal arrangement is very much of Empire influence. The piece has brown banding and black striping outlining major elements.

Although the overpainting makes certainty an impossibility, it appears that elements of the decora-

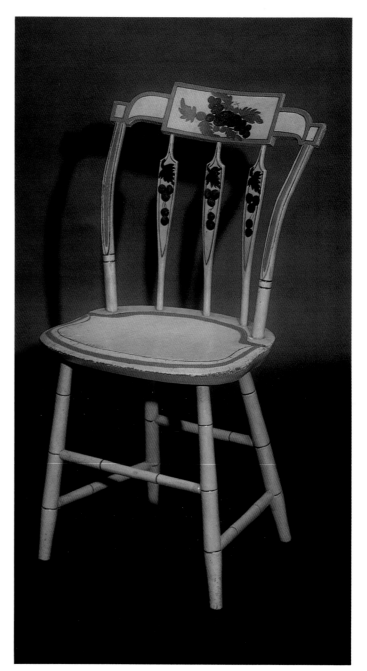

Figure 9: Capen chair. Courtesy of Lowell Innes.

tive motifs, and especially the fruit, may have been originally stenciled. This exemplifies a major shift occurring in decorated motifs during the first third of the nineteenth century. The earliest fancy chairs, like Federal furniture, were hand painted. However, by the 1810s, stenciled work was appearing on fine, often Empire furniture, and soon thereafter on less formal pieces, especially fancy chairs. With the perfection of bronze powder stenciling, and its promotion via the products of Lambert Hitchcock and contemporaries, stenciled chairs and other furniture forms quickly captured the market of the common man. Far simpler, quicker, and cheaper than free-hand painting, and very attractive, stenciling had everything in its favor.[27]

Figure 10: Hockey rocker. Courtesy of Arlie Porath.

A Salem rocker built by Joseph Hockey of Freedom, Maine (Fig. 10) in the late 1820s or early 1830s is almost wholly dependent on stencils for its major motifs. The leaves in the central tablet on the crest rail and in the flanking panels were applied with stencils. The only features that were executed freehand were the curlicues around the leaves and the fragile shrub in an ovoid panel centered on the front stretcher. The olive-green bands which frame the crest rail and the seat front accentuate the rocker. The reserved decoration is complemented by the form of the piece, especially the shaped seat, and the tall, sweeping back. The long spindles have inset ball turnings about a third of the way up, a feature characteristic of Maine chairs.[28]

Not surprisingly, the decorative format and motifs found on fancy chairs were applied to other furniture forms, a fact demonstrated by a washstand from the estate of Governor John Hubbard from Hallowell, Maine (Plate 8). Constructed ca. 1830, it is painted yellow with matching decorative motifs of fruit and foliage on the splashboard and drawer front. The melons, grapes, and leaves on the splashboard ears have been stenciled; conversely, the green leaves are handpainted, as are the black veins and curlicues. A combination of greenish-brown and olive-green bands, and black stripes effectively outline the major lines of the piece.

By the 1830s, decorated pieces with plain colored ground coats were being replaced by grained examples, the most frequent being red-and-black representing either mahogany or rosewood. Over this bronzed powder stencils were applied, usually in the form of a limited number of formalized and stylized motifs, especially bowls of fruit, and fruit and/or floral and foliage groupings.

A representative item is a box found in Skowhegan, Maine (Plate 20). Black-on-red grained, it has an elaborate stenciled suite, including a pair of fruit bowls on the front, one on the top, and one on each end, filled with an assortment of peaches, pears, pineapples, and pomegranates. Small, circular, narrow-petaled, round flowers accent and enclose the major groupings, and yellow curlicues with encircled hatch-marks frame the pineapple and pomegranate-filled bowl on the front. Mustard bands and yellow stripes complete the design.

The corners of the box top each contain a floral rosette. Similar rosettes frequently appear on pieces of this period (for example, see Plates 20 & 18). Unlike the majority of motifs on furniture of the period, these elements (as well as borders on some pieces, see Plate 19) were probably inspired by the metal ormolu used on Federal and Empire furniture.[29] The close relationship is underlined by the presence of actual brass rosettes on the South Paris bureau (Plate 12).

A set of four half-spindle thumb-back Windsors (ca. 1830s) acquired in Maine represent a typical decorative treatment (Plate 24). Black-on-red grained, their crest rails and central slats are each ornamented with a pair of large roses with appropriate foliage and buds. The chairs have inset balls turned into their spindles. The painted decorations are completed with green bands and yellow stripes, a combination found almost exclusively in central and west-central Maine.[30]

Of course, there were variations in decorative motifs, as evidenced on a late fancy side chair found in Thorndike, Maine (Plate 25). Black-on-red grained, it has a stenciled village complete with towers and a church centered on the yoke-shaped crest rail. The scene and flanking rosettes are enclosed by scrolling strapping, the top portion of which is now worn away. Strapping similarly outlines the shaped vase-back splat,

15

and an ornamented cartouche frames a vignette of a great cathedral. Finally, a complex lace-like stencil pattern graces the back posts. More than many pieces, this chair mirrors its Empire heritage in the yoke crest and vase splat, but most especially in the European-style scenic and architectural motifs and the flower rosettes on the crest rail ears.

By mid-century, furniture construction and decorative patterns had become more simplified due in large part to the strictures imposed by the rapidly establishing factory system. In order to produce quantities of furniture inexpensively and quickly, complexities had to be minimized. Many factory-made pieces, especially of the inexpensive sort, received a solid monocolor ground coat. One-piece stencils were used, and such embellishments as shading and depth-of-field disappeared. Striping declined both in quantity and quality. These techniques, combined with labor- and time-saving construction processes, culminated in the production of a large volume of inexpensive furniture. Not quite as elegant as that made earlier, it was still fairly attractive and it was cheap.

The factory system was clearly moving into place in Maine by mid-nineteenth century. Besides the large Corey firm in Portland employing nearly one hundred people, there were a number of smaller operations. F.J. and C.A. Rollins of Berwick employed twelve people, and John Mullay and A. Dole & Co. of Bangor, Samuel Haley of Bath, and Luke Brown of Bridgton had operations with ten workers apiece. There were also twenty-one other firms utilizing between four and nine employees.[31]

A small late-Windsor armless rocker made by John Meservey typifies the inexpensive furniture of the 1840s (Fig. 11). Of the simplest construction, it is black painted and has single-piece stenciled patterns on the crest rail and the seat front. Striping has been limited to the same two areas. Interestingly, Meservey was a fairly small operator; however, to be competitive with Mullay, Dole, and others in town plus similar operations elsewhere, Meservey had to make the same shortcuts as his larger competitors.

There are always items which do not fit any standard patterns. Some are imaginative and, at times, novel extensions of familiar forms and techniques; others seem wholly new, the products of pure individual creativity. Although small in number, these objects attract a great deal of attention, for, through them, craft has become art. Even so, they must be seen in perspective. Like the highlights of a painting, they accent but must not dominate the story of Maine's decorated furniture, for they focus on individual productions rather than the broader subject.

Still, for all the caveats, we are drawn to these pieces like magnets, and two objects have a very special attraction. A blanket chest with "New Portland" scrawled across the top (Plate 9) and a matching box (Plate 9) exemplify the capabilities of a gifted

Figure 11: Meservey rocker. MSM photograph. Present location unknown.

and inventive decorator who could transform a common furniture form with bronze stencils and black-on-red graining. The graining undulates across the blanket chest and curls in whirling scrolls across the box. On both, stencils unlike any others elaborate the flat surfaces. The chest top is bordered with stags and dogs alternating in frozen pursuit, and the box front features a wolf and a fox poised in mid-bound after a pair of startled rabbits, themselves leaping toward a centered schematic bush (briar patch?). Supplementing these images are several other stencils that all but defy description. The major motif, centered on the box top and chest front, has a geometric lyre from which scroll two stylized cornucopia issuing forth what look like reversed thistles. The whole is underlaid with outward flowing vines. This composition is flanked by a pair of motifs that rise from a base into a rounded multi-element unit that can best be described as pure design. Add to these diamonds, schematic baskets, and pointing-finger hands, and the result is an object without peer.

Daniel Stewart from Farmington, one of Maine's foremost chairmakers, was responding to a far different influence when he decorated a set of six step-down Windsors (Plate 23). After constructing the chairs, Stewart gave them a salmon-colored ground coat and then decorated them in patterns that clearly reflect the painting contemporaneously being done on tinware.[32] The motif on the crest rail is especially reminiscent, with the central red ball and flanking paired sets of brush stroke green and red leaves. The same spirit echoes in the set of alternately red-and-green brush stroke leaves on the front stretcher, the elongated teardrops on the legs and spindles, and the dotted accents framing various elements. Finally, through the use of red-and-green striping and the red bordered green band around the seat, Stewart even provides these common elements of a decorated chair with a special presence.

The Stewart chairs have an interesting, albeit rather convoluted and conjectural, association with a small green box (Plate 22). The box has a series of stamped white diamonds in light olive green bands rimming the top, front, and sides. It also has freehand red-accented vining leaves and berry clusters meandering along the base molding.

Of special interest is the fact that the stamped diamonds appear to have been applied with the same tool that was used to decorate a pair of chairs with a long provenance to Livermore, Maine.[33] Therefore, it would seem that the individual who decorated the box probably decorated the chairs. The final item worthy of note is that the Livermore chairs have a marked resemblance to the Stewart examples made in Farmington, less than twenty miles away. There is no way at this point to verify whether Stewart actually made the chairs; however, whoever made the Livermore pieces was operating with the same design vocabulary.

In spite of their originality and inventiveness, the decorators of the New Portland chest, the Stewart chair, and the earlier-noted decorated yellow chest simply cannot compare to the painter of a fantastic small green box found in Augusta (Plate 22). A pair of yellow-decorated, red-lobed pinwheels with extending leaves and flowers appear on the front while a third centers the top, and strange semicircular multicolored baskets reverse the order of the pinwheels on the two surfaces. The front top edge is decorated with acorns and red-veined yellow leaves, and small red balls sit at each corner of the ends. Finally, red-and-black striping and yellow banding outline the form of the piece.

As if to mystify the viewer, the cryptic text "Jn X C.y X 1835" is painted on the back. Two papers lining the box corroborate the date and geographic origins of the item. One, dated October 20, 1834, is a broadside by Dr. Alexander Hatch of Augusta, advertising drugs and medicine. The second is part of an unidentified 1835 Hallowell newspaper, on which the latest advertisements are dated January 9, 1835. The maker of this piece may well remain anonymous and the inspiration for the piece remain unknown. However, the imaginative singularity of the creator of the box cannot be denied; by any definition, this is a unique object.

Turning from the exceptional to the typical, an always intriguing question is whether there are any statewide, regional, or local patterns in the utilization of specific or general decorative motifs. Two general features appear with some frequency on Maine painted furniture. The first is the use of green, especially olive green, both in banding and on ornamental groupings. Although not unique to Maine, this color appears with surprising frequency on pieces provenanced to the State. The second is the use of bright, contrasting colors for striping and banding, including such combinations as red, yellow and black (Plate 22), red and green (Plates 6, 13, 23), and yellow and green (Plates 12, 24, 25, 30, etc.).

Looking to more regionalized or localized patterns, probably the best known pattern is red-and-black graining with green banding and yellow striping. With but two exceptions, all documented or attributable pieces come from central or west central Maine and none has been traced to non-Maine origins. Another pattern which has been tentatively identified is an ochre yellow, brown and green sponge graining (Plate 11). A number of pieces so decorated have been found in Solon and nearby communities; however, more research will be necessary before this combination is verified as a local or regional phenomenon.

Still, the most interesting pattern involves less a specific combination than an overall pattern of decorative mindsets. A survey of the pieces in the exhibition supports a general impression that variations do exist within the State. In roughest terms, there are at least three major regions. In the southwestern part of the State (including Portland) the decoration tends to be formal and sophisticated. To the northeast in Washington and Hancock counties, there is a decided lack of decorated furniture and that which does exist tends to be reserved and understated. However, sandwiched between these two areas is a region incorporating the Kennebec and Androscoggin river drainages. In this area, something very different was going on. The overwhelming number of strikingly and often exotically-decorated pieces of Maine furniture came out of this area.

The obvious question is "why?" The answer seems to be a mixture of politics, class structure, religion, and geography.[34] Southwestern Maine is an area that was politically, socially, and religiously conservative in the first half of the nineteenth-century. The longest settled area in the region, it was the bastion of Whigs and Congregationalists, and contained the vast majority of well-to-do residing in the State. The region looked to Boston for its role models, and the furnishings produced and used by the people in the area often reflected the desire to emulate the sophistication of the Bay capital. Obviously, not all inhabitants responded so simply to urban models, especially those in non-coastal towns; still, southwestern Maine was not the breeding place for radicals.

At the other end, in northeastern Maine, a wholly different circumstance prevailed. The region had been recently settled, and the inhabitants were generally poor, isolated from the metropolitan areas, and never far from the wilderness. Stoic Calvinists and conservatives, these were not people with the desire or opportunity to produce dramatic, brightly decorated furniture — and they didn't.

Central and west-central Maine represented yet a third situation. The region had not been settled very long and it, too, was less than wealthy. However, the inhabitants were not so close to the cutting edge of poverty, and they had frequent relations with neighbors (often wealthy) to the south regarding trade, land, and politics. The lack of isolation created a sense of security not present to the northeast; however, land feuds and a variety of other quarrels turned the people of the region into Populist Democrats. They also flocked to Free-will Baptist, Methodist, and other new sectarian churches and participated in impassioned revivals. It is from this atmosphere and these people that our most vividly decorated furniture descended.

Detail of top of Kents Hill table (Pl. 2). Collection of George Morrill, Harrison, Maine.

18

Section II.

The Decorators

Unfortunately, the decorators of Maine's painted furniture did little to help in the identification of their work. Unlike makers who sometimes signed individual items, few decorators ever did so unless they were also the builders. When signed pieces of painted furniture are found, it can be presumed that the signature is that of the cabinetmaker or owner, not the decorator. There are a substantial number of instances where the maker and the decorator were one and the same, but there is no way to prove this by reference to the furniture itself.

Still, decorative painters can be documented in such sources as census records and city directories. Included in this group are John Trask, cabinetmaker and painter of Portland; Orin Parker, chair trimmer of Augusta; and Nelson Holt of Bangor who "manufactured and painted furniture."[1] However, these sources share the major shortcomings that individuals are too often simply listed as "painters." Undoubtedly some, if not many, of these individuals were capable of executing ornamental painting, but until more data is available there is no way to demonstrate that to be the situation.

Newspaper advertisements offer the best preliminary source of information on decorators, both in terms of identity and type of work being done. Typical examples include: an 1822 advertisement by John Gilman of Hallowell noting that he did chaise, coach, sign and house painting as well as gilding, glazing and varnishing;[2] an 1846 notice by N.A. and S.H. Burpee of East Thomaston stating they did "house, ship, sign and ornamental" painting;[3] and an 1856 item by Isaac Frazier of Ellsworth, indicating he did house, ship, sign and ornamental painting, paying "particular attention. . . to graining, varnishing, polishing, ornamenting and enameling."[4]

The question still remains as to which of the individuals who advertised actually decorated furniture. For example, in 1823, Belfast painters Nicholas Phillips and Thomas Flagner stated that they were "carrying on HOUSE, SHIP AND SIGN PAINTING," and would "also paint MASONIC FLOORING AND APRONS, Tablets for Looking Glasses and other Painting on Glass and [would execute] chair painting. . . with care, accuracy, and neatness."[5] Even more to the point were Micah and Hiram Safford, Augusta decorators who in 1831 claimed they would "carry on the Chair making, Painting and Glazing business in all its branches."[6] Others such as John Meservey of Bangor were a bit less direct, but no less clearly involved in furniture decoration. In 1832 he advertised the manufacture of a "good. . . assortment of CHAIRS" and that "SIGN & FANCY PAINTING [would be] done at short notice."[7] John Daggett of Portland ran a similar ad only a few years earlier.[8]

As noted above, though, many decorators who advertised did not indicate that they painted furniture. Undoubtedly some did not; on the other hand, some almost certainly did. For a number of individuals, advertisements provide an important indirect connection. For example, John Gilman of Hallowell was doing his chaise and sign painting, gilding, and varnishing in the shop occupied by John Brown, a chair manufacturer.[9] In and of itself, this physical proximity is not conclusive; however, the same connection between decorator and furniture maker is revealed in the advertisements of John Treworthy and Charles Chamberlain of Ellsworth, Israel Cleaves of Saco, Lewis Sargent of Hallowell, and Amaziah Moore and Horatio Beale of Bangor.[10] Providing even more evidence of this pattern is the example of John B. Hudson of Portland, who was employed as a painter for a furniture maker after having an earlier career as a chairmaker and fancy painter.[11]

But there are still a substantial number of individuals for whom no such relationships are suggested. However, further research through such sources as deeds, probate records, directories, and censuses often will provide significant data regarding the roles of these individuals in furniture decoration as well as a number of other pertinent questions. An impressive example

Figure 12: Jepheth Beale. Courtesy of Green Street Methodist Church, Augusta, Maine.

of what can be developed is exemplified in an examin-ation of the activities of the Beale group of painters from Augusta and Bangor.

Three Beales, Horatio, Jepheth, and Oliver Salem arrived in Augusta during the first quarter of the nineteenth century. The latter two were brothers, and while Horatio's relationship to them is not known, there are bits of evidence which suggests a tie.[12] Horatio appeared in Augusta in 1824 where, on July 10, he purchased a parcel of land, the transaction being witnessed by Amaziah Moore, his future partner, who then lived in Sidney. At that time both men listed themselves as painters.[13] The following year Horatio and Moses Wells of Augusta, listing themselves as cabinetmakers, acquired another piece of property.[14]

At about that time, Horatio and Amaziah moved to Bangor, for in May of 1825 they had established themselves in a partnership in that city. The two men advertised painting and, later, chairmaking, finally dis-solving the relationship in November, 1828.[16] Both continued individually after that, with Beale building and decorating chairs and Moore practicing decorative painting.[17] Beale divested himself of Augusta property once he moved to Bangor. One transaction is of special interest though. On August 21, 1828, Horatio sold a tract of land to Augusta chairmaker Elihu Robinson. Robinson was a close friend, and eventually a partner, of Jepheth Beale.[18]

Jepheth and Oliver Salem Beale had both arrived in the Augusta area from Bridgewater, Massachusetts, in the early nineteenth century, where they had been born in 1781 and 1776 respectively.[19] Jepheth (Fig. 12) appears early in the records as a housewright, and then in 1814 as a chairmaker.[20] The following two decades, he refers to himself as a yeoman or husband-man.[21] In 1836, he identifies himself as a painter for the first time, and soon after he has allied with cabinet-maker Elihu Robinson, a partnership which seems to have lasted for a couple of years.[22] After that, he continued on his own as a painter until near his death in 1863.[23]

Jepheth's son Chandler, born in 1817, continued his father's trade.[24] In 1846, he advertised that he and partner Joshua L. Heath were carrying on house, ship, and sign painting, and that they could also do "grain-ing of all descriptions."[25] Although both men were painters, they were still interested in employing a specialist, for in 1848 they said they were "prepared to do graining in as good styles as can be done on the River, having in their employment a person experi-enced in that kind of work who has had practice in Boston and Lowell."[26] The partnership lasted into the early 1850s but probably ended by mid-decade. Chandler worked alone for a short time, but by 1857 apparently was in partnership with another Augusta painter, Joseph Farnham.[27]

The third early Beale, Oliver Salem, arrived in the region during the first decade of the nineteenth century. After spending time in such neighboring towns as Monmouth, Sidney, Hallowell, and Readfield, he had established himself in Augusta by 1829.[28] On September 24, 1830, he published his first advertisement, informing readers that he would "be happy to execute all orders in the various branches of sign, chaise, and fancy painting and gilding."[29] Two months later, he detailed how he could paint "in imitation of wood, such as mahogany, oak, birch, maple, & c. — also Thomaston, Egyptian, and Italian marble, done in the neatest style."[30] Two years later, Oliver was expanding his activities, offering "Prime waggons for sale."[31] Not long after, he moved to Bangor and by 1843 he was building carriages with partner William Osgood. The connection was shortlived; by mid-decade, Oliver was back painting. He also listed himself as a daguerreotypist in 1846; but that avenue apparently proved wanting, and in 1848 Oliver Salem Beale had returned to carriage and sign painting, an activity which he continued until he disappeared from Bangor city directories in the mid-1850s.[32]

In reviewing the activities of the Beale decorators, the most prominent feature is the clear relationship between decorators, furniture makers, and vehicle builders — patterns already suggested earlier. Jepheth and Horatio Beale, and Horatio's partner Amaziah Moore, all made and painted furniture, and were involved with other chair and furniture makers. Jepheth's son, Chandler, was closely tied with his father as well as other painters, including George W. Snow, Joseph Farnham, and Joshua Heath, who was himself involved in transactions with Augusta cabinet-maker David Knowlton.[33] Oliver Salem Beale seemed more focused on sign and vehicle painting; still, he acquired his sign boards from Knowlton[34] and, considering the frequent liaisons between carriage painters and furniture builders, he probably decorated a few pieces during his career.

Also of interest are the strong ties of the Beales and their association with the newly-established Methodist church in Maine. Oliver Salem Beale arrived in the Kennebec Valley in 1801 and spent nearly thirty years as an itinerant minister to Readfield, Hallowell, and a number of other communities. In 1829, he was established for a year in the pulpit of the newly built Methodist Church in Augusta, Maine. After that he was highly active in Augusta and later Bangor in church affairs, both local and statewide.[35]

Oliver's brother Jepheth had a major role in Augusta's Methodist community. In 1802, he founded the first class (the local organizational unit) in the town. Over the next several decades, he and Elihu Robinson led the four local classes, held numerous meetings, and were key in establishing the Methodist Church as an ongoing institution in Augusta.[36]

A further indication of sentiment within the Beale and associates group is provided by Amaziah S. Moore, partner of Horatio Beale. On April 7, 1828, Moore put a tract of land in Sidney in trust to the local Methodist Wesleyan Society. An action taken after he moved to Bangor along with Horatio, he, nonetheless, continued a strong concern for the Methodist church in his previous community.[37]

William Capen, Jr., of Portland, provides a somewhat different image than did the Beales of Augusta and Bangor. Apparently the only family member who worked as a decorative painter, he generally maintained his independent status, only once forming a partnership with painter John Carr in the mid-1830s.[38] Born in Portland in 1802, Capen was listed as a chairmaker in the 1823 directory, and the year following was advertising himself as a chairmaker and painter.[39] In 1826, William was secure enough in his situation to join the Maine Charitable Mechanics Association and to marry Miss Anne H. Walton, also of Portland.[40] Only a year later, Capen gave up chairmaking, going to full-time painting, including the repainting of old chairs.[41] From then on, his reputation as a sign painter grew, until around mid-century he began suffering from "painter's colic."[42] This left him in fragile health through the 1840s, and when he died in 1863, Capen had not had use of his legs for several years.[43] "Painter's colic" was a well known affliction, having already been described in 1713 by Bernardini Romazzini, the first serious scholar of occupational illnesses, in his *De Morbis Artificum (Disease of Workers)*. His description of the painters' affliction follows:

> Painters. "I have observed that nearly all the painters who I know, both in this and other cities, are sickly; and if one reads the lives of painters it will be seen that they are by no means long-lived, especially those who were most distinguished... For their liability to disease there is a more immediate cause, I mean the materials of the colors they handle and smell constantly, such as red lead, cinnabar, white lead, varnish, nut-oil and linseed oil which they use for mixing colors; and the numberous pigments made of various mineral substances."[44]

The real villains, of course, were lead and other heavy metal compounds in the paint. Lead affects the gastrointestinal system, red blood cells, and neuromuscular system. The results include intestinal disorders, weakening of extremities, headaches, irritability, malaise, muscle and joint pains, and liver and kidney damage.[45] Unfortunately, Capen was probably only one of many decorators who ended their careers and lives in the grip of lead, mercury, or related toxins.

An individual with a somewhat healthier career, Nathaniel Knowlton of Eliot was a cabinetmaker and carriagemaker who also did some painting. Born on May 6, 1791, to John and Dorcus Knowlton,[46] he next appeared in 1812 working for the Boston cabinet-maker Benjamin Lamson. In Lamson's employ, he constructed substantial quantities of formal furniture, often of mahogany.[47]

In 1815, Knowlton set up on his own in Eliot, carrying on cabinet-making and, increasingly, carriage-making. His furniture was not as sophisticated as Lamson's, usually being constructed of birch, maple, pine, basswood, and not a little quantity of cherry.[48] He was constructing some fairly handsome pieces, including "a Swelled Bureau Cherry Front"; "a bureau, mahogany front, top projected, turned and reeded pillars"; and "a Cherrytree Desk."[49] Still, most of his furniture was far plainer, including "a birch bureau," "a small table," "a straight-front bureau," etc.[50]

Although not in great numbers, Knowlton was also producing painted furniture. Several times he mentioned "making a chest and painting"; he also noted constructing and painting cradles, sinks, a clock case, and a picture frame.[51] Meanwhile, he was building and painting substantial numbers of wagons, sleighs, and chaises.[52]

As Knowlton's career progressed, he gradually shifted more and more to vehicle manufacture and painting. In terms of painting, the reason is evident when one compares the income derived from painting furniture with that of painting vehicles. For repairing and painting six chairs Knowlton earned $2.25; for painting a closet, 75¢; for painting a chest and putting on a lock, 37½¢; for painting two tables and a cradle, 65¢; and for varnishing fourteen chairs, a bureau, and a desk, $1.25.[53] On the other hand, painting sleighs, chaises and wagons brought in $2.50 to $4.00 apiece.[54] This was clearly fancy work, for to simply give a wagon a coat of paint only cost 75¢.[55] Furthermore, Knowlton at least once documented doing decorative painting — charging 25¢ for striping a chaise spring.[56]

Knowlton also did a fair amount of house painting and wallpapering. However, like furniture painting, this was not an overly lucrative activity. He earned a dollar or less for a day's work, and about 75¢ per room. Wallpapering was in about the same category, with Knowlton earning $1.00 a day for papering in the house of Thomas Goodwin, and $2.00 to paint and paper Nathaniel Goodwin's home.[57]

As mid-century came, Nathaniel was slowing down. He handled a decreasing number of customers and in the 1850 census listed himself as a farmer, even though the last entry in his account book was made in 1859.[58] Knowlton died four years later, apparently leaving a modestly respectable estate, if his 1850 census real estate valuation of $1500 is indicative.[59]

Whereas Knowlton's career was quietly successful, that of Isaac R. Park of Bangor, seems anything but.

At this point, the only detailed knowledge of Park extends from 1825 to 1829, but during that four-year period, he convincingly demonstrated his capacity for misfortune and an inability to grasp the fundamentals of his chosen craft.

He first appeared with E. L. Park (brother?) in March 17, 1825 when they advertised that "by strict attention to business, and their experiences in house, sign, and ornamental painting and glazing, they hope to meet a share of the approbation and encouragement of a generous public."[60]

The partnership lasted until midsummer, after which Isaac continued the business that he and E. L. had established. By the next spring, besides facing the common malady of outstanding bills, he had already created a new problem for himself by loaning out the tools of his trade. He asked that those who had borrowed his "Staging, Ladders, Brushes, Paint Buckets and other Tools" return them "forthwith" and save him and them trouble.[61]

The situation further deteriorated as Park, shortly after, fell ill. He had recovered by June; however, his business problems worsened. In late December he demanded that all those with outstanding debts or who still had his tools had better settle affairs by February 20, or have their accounts turned over to a law firm. Meanwhile, he was pleading for the "further continuance of his old Patrons, and a new set to call on him."[62] By the next spring, he was so frustrated about his illusive equipment that he was offering rewards to anyone who could tell him where the items could be found.[63]

If this weren't enough, Park's wife, Sally, had apparently lost interest in her husband, for on January 16, 1828, he announced that Sally had participated in "a long course of indecent and unbecoming conduct" and had "forsaken my bed and board." Thereafter, he would not be responsible for her debts.[64] This would not be the last advertisement on the problem. One can't quite be sure which of the above difficulties finally brought the change, but by the spring of 1828, Park had quit painting and was putting on roofs. That certainly did not resolve his problems, because he almost went over the Bangor Falls to his death, but for the timely assistance of some local inhabitants.[65]

Still, one cannot keep a good man down. In November, 1829, Park was back advertising that he was doing house, sign, and ornamental painting, glazing and varnishing. He also cut glass in various forms for ornamental windows, whitewashed rooms, hung papers, and cemented around chimneys and leaky gutters. He then

> flatter[ed] himself that he can work superior to what he could do two or three years ago; and that his exertions to make improvements on what he already knows of the above business, by application and strict attention to it, and his abhorrence of what is misnamed "O be joyful"

[i.e., alcohol], will obtain for him a liberal patronage.[66]

Soon thereafter, Isaac moved to Dixfield, Maine, where in 1850 he was still living, although with a new wife, Emeline. Apparently he had given up the painting business, for he was listing himself as a carpenter. Amazingly, he had been able to accumulate $2,000 worth of real estate.[67] A new spouse and a new occupation seemed to have done him well.

Looking back at the Beales, Capen, and other painters mentioned above, and at the products of Maine decorators, known and unknown, the one thing that is most impressive is the diversity. There was a decorator family, a renowned sign and fancy painter, a cabinetmaker for whom painting was only a sideline, and a man who finally had the good sense to get out of the business and take up another trade. In terms of wares, the painter of the New Portland blanket chest (Plate 9) showed imagination and creativity which was light years beyond the simplified decorations that John Meservey of Bangor used on his little rocker (Fig. 11). And there were different mindsets: the chair painter for Walter Corey was carefully producing a controlled, sophisticated product (Plate 27), whereas the decorator of the Rumford bureau (Plate 13) felt few restraints in his mix of colors, patterns, and techniques.

Still, there was some commonality among decorators. For one thing, it seems that most came from the economic and social middle and lower classes. Twenty-one decorators active at mid-century were located in the 1850 census. Of those, only nine indicated that they owned any real estate; four were furniture makers as well, and claimed the highest worth — from $1,500 to $15,000. The five painters with real estate held property valued at $175, $250, $600, $1,600, and $3,500 respectively. The wealthiest individual was famous chair and sign painter William Capen, who had also been able to supplement his wealth with a brief career as a custom inspector. The other twelve painters, including cabinetmaker-painter Joseph Simonds, had no recorded real estate.[68]

That decorators were not able to amass great quantities of money is not surprising considering the economics of their trade. Unless they combined furniture, vehicle, or another type of construction with decoration, they were providing the least profitable aspect of creating an object. This situation was exacerbated in terms of furniture, for as noted regarding Nathaniel Knowlton, painting chairs, chests, and tables was one of the least profitable aspects of this trade. Considering the fact that the furniture being decorated was generally the most inexpensive being produced, the profit margin was small and the cabinetmaker could neither pay a painter much nor add significantly to his own cost if he did the painting himself.

Many decorators, like Knowlton, moved to other types of painting that offered better profits; and others, such as Park, found new occupations. Then there were those who moved into major furniture firms where they obtained skilled and semi-skilled jobs as ornamental painters. Francis Holland, George Lord, and Andrew Elliot all settled in with the Walter Corey operation, and Warren Phillips and Daniel Carr found employment with Portland chairmakers Todd and Beckett.[69] A regular wage probably seemed a pleasant prospect and, according to George Lord, a good worker could make $3.00 a day shortly after mid-century.[70] Considering that Nathaniel Knowlton was earning $1.00 per day painting in the 1830s and 1840s, such a wage had to be viewed quite favorably.

Besides modest wages, painters faced the ever-present threat of "painter's colic." An affliction which affected many members of the trade to some degree, it left all under the continued fear of premature disabilities and, ultimately, death.

The life of the decorator had its disadvantages, and probably most parents would have selected a different career for their children. Still, there were some painters who did well and for most, the trade probably provided a decent living. And, to our benefit, they left behind a body of artifacts that will ever brighten our world just as they brightened that of our ancestors.

Advertisement for Oliver Salem Beale of Augusta in the [Augusta] Maine *Patriot and State Gazette*, November 17, 1830.

Examples of painted grains frequently seen in Maine: Red/Black (upper left); Bird's Eye Maple (center); Maple (upper right); Rosewood (lower left); Mahogany (lower right).

Section III.

Techniques in Decoration

An Overview on Methods of Nineteenth Century Graining

By Stephen Weston

Furniture made of wood has usually been finished in some manner for both aesthetic and protective reasons. Among the various finishes used, graining and decorative painting gained its widest favor during the first half of the nineteenth century in Maine.

Paints, colored finishes, and stains are all similar. All consist of a vehicle, a binder and pigments. For example the ''red stain'' finish, used to great extent on Maine birch furniture, consisted simply of varnish colored with red pigments. The varnish bound the pigment and the alcohol in which the varnish was dissolved was the vehicle or thinner that allowed the colored finish to be applied as a liquid with a brush. Similarly, oil paint used linseed oil and turpentine as a vehicle and white lead as a binder. The oil also helped bind the paint and the white lead acted as a white pigment base which could be tinted with other pigments to determine the color.

Painted furniture often was simply referred to as ''decorated,'' a term which covered furniture finished in a variety of techniques and effects. Some were done ''wet'', i.e. while the paints or glazes involved were still wet. Other methods were done ''dry'', one layer after another after each had dried. Wet painting took advantage of the results gained when wet paint ran slightly after being manipulated. Still other types of decoration were plain painted and enhanced by the addition of such things as striping and stenciling.

Graining, or the imitation of wood grain with paint, when done using ''wet'' techniques, was quite sophisticated. It required the greatest skill and produced the best results — often being nearly indistinguishable from the real wood it copied. The commonly imitated woods were mahogany and, to a lesser extent, rosewood. Occasionally satinwood and figured maple were done also.

The first step was the preparation of the surface by application of a ground coat of paint. One or more coats were applied until a smooth surface was established. Mahogany graining was done on a white-lead ground that had been tinted pink by the addition of red pigment. Rosewood and maple graining was done on a plain white ground color.

The second step was covering the now-dry ground color with a glaze and manipulating it to get the effect of wood grain. Glazes seem to have been oil based. They were usually somewhat transparent and consisted of linseed oil, perhaps a small amount of white lead as a dryer, and the necessary pigments. For mahogany a dark brown glaze was brushed on over the pink ground and then brushed and wiped off to show greater and lesser amounts of ground color. This produced the basic areas of light and dark shading, and established the overall grain pattern such as that imitating crotch veneer. Then additional glazes, including often several of darker tones, were worked into the still wet first glaze to detail it. Most often a brush was used to simply draw in the grain. The wet glazes ran together producing a soft effect very much like the blended tones and figure of real mahogany. After drying, the surface was given several coats of shellac to make a highly finished surface (Fig. 13).

Rosewood graining was done similarly, but more often appears to have made use of irregular combs to ''rake'' the glazes into grain patterns. Combs were simply stiff paper, leather or even pieces of tin with notches cut along the edge. When used to ''drag off'' or ''rake'' a glaze they left alternating lines of glazed and unglazed areas. This type of decoration was used primarily on the cases of keyboard instruments (Fig. 3 and Plate 27).

Maple was imitated by using a yellow-brown glaze over a white ground color. Tiger maple figure was done by ''pushing'' the glaze into ridges of deeper color using a piece of cloth or leather. Bird's-eye maple figure was made by picking the wet glaze up into dots with a straw or stick (Plates 5 and 31). Often maple graining was done in two steps. First a simple wood grain pattern was brushed on and then the figure was added either directly to this still-wet

Figure 13: Hubbard Estate commode, Hallowell. MSM collection.

first glaze or done in a second glaze applied after the first had dried (Fig. 14). Maple graining was done on woodwork as well as furniture such as on the drawer fronts of figured maple graining used in red-stained cases that were prominent elements of the Sheraton and Empire style in Maine.

Wet graining was also done in other combinations of colors, particularly red and yellow. Some examples of this color seem to have been done by working the red into a still-wet yellow ground color.

A common adjunct to "wet" graining was the use of a "drag line" to stripe the piece. This was done by dragging a stick through the wet paint or glaze to create a line. This was a simple way to imitate a line of inlay. Examples exist where this technique was used to write words in the decorated surface before it dried (Plates 5 and 21).

Sponge and "seaweed" decorating were also "wet" techniques. Similar results were obtained by several different methods. True "seaweed" decoration was supposedly done by first applying a glaze containing

vinegar over a ground coat, then gathering the glaze up into patterns with a piece of putty containing a little oil. As the glaze dried the oil and vinegar separated forming the seaweed appearance. Few extant examples seem to be of this technique. Although this method, or more likely a variation of it, was apparently used successfully, examples of it are uncommon probably because other ways to get almost the same effects were much easier. Simple sponge graining, the dabbing of paint over a ground color with a piece of crumpled paper or leather, was used occasionally. By far the commonest mode, however, was to first brush the glaze over the ground color, then press a piece of paper or leather into it to work the glaze up into rows and circle patterns. The puckered effect caused by theglaze being gathered up by the leather was distinctive.

A wide range of colors were used in sponge grain-ing. The most often used was an ochre-brown over a light yellow or white ground color. Less common were green over yellow, red over yellow, blue over white, and black over white. These all seem to have been done with an oil-based glaze over a white lead and oil-based ground coat. This type of decoration, as with most others, was finished with a top coat of varnish to brighten the colors and give the piece a gloss (Plates 11, 14, 17 and 21).

"Dry" graining, although it could be elaborate, was usually a simple and somewhat primitive method of decoration. The common black and red graining was done using this method (Plates 7, 10 and 18). Although usually referred to as black over red, a number of Maine examples are actually red over black (Plate 27). In either case it was most often done in varnish-based paints. These were somewhat transparent and thin, sometimes not being much more than stains that colored the wood rather than covering it. After laying on the ground color and letting it dry, the top color was brushed on in the desired pattern. Many pieces of Maine furniture were grained in red and black and then striped in a fine yellow strip and a wider green stripe (Plates 24 and 32).

"Dry" graining was done in other colors besides red and black. Black over white, black over brown and various ochre yellow and brown combinations were used also (Plate 21). Some of these paints were oil-based rather than varnish based.

Figure 14:   Hubbard Estate commode, Hallowell. MSM collection.

"Dry" graining was also the method of choice for decorating the vast numbers of fancy chairs and their descendants that were made in Maine in the nineteenth century. Varnish-based black over red was very common. The black was often just roughly brushed over the red in a rather haphazard manner, leaving lots of red showing through. Later chairs of the Empire style, such as fiddle-back chairs, were often grained black over brown in fine brush strokes. Some were even grained in black directly on the raw or slightly stained wood surface. Some late chairs may have been given the same effect by using an acid instead of black paint to darken the wood in a grained patern. These various colors and types of graining were almost invariably striped in various colors and often served as bases for elaborate stenciling and free hand work. All were topped of with varnish to brighten them (Plates 20, 26 and 27).

Much of what we call decorated furniture was not grain-painted but simply painted in plain colors and decorated by various techniques. One of the most interesting was "smoke graining." Most often used on a yellow or white ground, it was also used on grey/green painted clock doors and even on bare wood and rocking horses. A lamp or candle was used to make the dark patterns by holding it close under the surface to be smoked and moving it around in the desired design (Plates 3 and 13).

Other furniture was decorated by hand-painting it with brush work designs similar to those used on tin articles or by striping it in various bands and lines of varied colors.

All of the decorative techniques show a great variety of skills and various levels of success. Many combinations of methods and colors were used by decorators seemingly trying to achieve ever more spectacular results. In so doing they went far beyond the simple requirements that a finish be aesthetic and protective.

Detail of stencil on New Portland box (Pl. 9) Maine State Museum.

A Brief Treatise on the History and Execution of Bronze Stenciling

By Kenneth Jewett

When we contemplate nineteenth-century stenciled work, we must consider the history of two specific elements — lacquering and stenciling. Lacquering evolved in the Orient for the decoration of numerous objects. In the seventeenth century, England and Europe became fascinated with the lacquered items coming from the Far East, and soon began trying to copy the process. However, they had problems. The base for Chinese and Japanese lacquer came from cuts in the bark of a special tree, while those in India used the encrustations of insects mixed with spirits (alcohol).[1] In search for a substitute, the English and Europeans developed a variation made with resin lac dissolved in methylated industrial spirits.[2] The English, who were leading importers of Oriental work, and were very interested in learning the various techniques for doing lacquer work, had by the eighteenth century become quite proficient in this art.[3]

The best early lacquer work was being exported by Japan, where gold powder was used.[4] However, an increase in product demand forced the Japanese to use powders made from grindings of pure metals, alloys, and other materials. One such combination may have been what we now term bronze powder.[5] Thomas Hubbal and Charles Valentine, between 1812 and 1819, were among the first in England to use bronze powders.[6] These powdered bronzes came in shades of gold, silver, brass and bronze.

The art of lacquering had moved west from the Orient, while that of stenciling probably developed in several places across the globe, including early Europe. Still, the trigger for the rapid spread of this skill in the western world seems to have been a second Oriental discovery — papermaking. Developed in China, the process traveled west through Baghdad, Egypt, Japan, Spain, Morocco, Constantinople, reaching Italy by 1276. The introduction of papermaking into medieval Europe dramatically expanded the use of the stencil. Utilized in the making of playing cards

as early as the 1500s, stenciled decorations were increasingly applied to an ever broader list of objects, including posters, banners, and wallpapers.[7]

It was only a matter of time before japanning, bronze powders, and stencils would come together. The vehicle proved to be the vast quantity of decorated tinplated ware that was being produced in Pontypool, Wales, and nearby towns from the late seventeenth century. In the late eighteenth and early nineteenth centuries, bronze-powdered stenciled motifs began joining the rich designs gracing the elaborate trays and other wares.[8]

Bronze stenciled designs were soon used on other forms, including furniture, and by the early nineteenth century had been introduced in America, appearing c. 1815 on pieces of formal New York Empire furniture. The practice, because of its low cost and ease of application, was soon applied to less formal pieces as a substitute for hand painting and expensive ormolu.

Popularized by Lambert Hitchcock in the 1820s and 1830s, stenciling was soon widely used by American furniture ornamentors.[9] Most of the early stencilers remain anonymous, although the names and work of a few have come down to us including Jared Johnson, Reuben Goodrich, Ives and William White, Thomas Gildersleeve, Ramson Cook, and William P. Eaton.[10] The delicacy of Eaton's stencils quite surpassed that of his contemporaries.

In Maine, the best-known furniture decorator and stenciler, and a great admirer of W. P. Eaton's work, was George Lord (1833-1929). In 1848, at age fifteen, Lord, whose father had been a cabinetmaker, became an apprentice to Francis Holland, a furniture decorator at the Walter Corey furniture factory in Portland. His aptitude and dedication to his work brought rapid promotions. Lord became proficient in graining, striping, and stenciling. He was made foreman at an early age. Through the years, Lord copied as many patterns of the early masters as possible, especially those of W. P. Eaton. He continued his interest in stenciling and was an active decorator well into his eighties. Although most of his work postdated the Golden Age of Stenciling, he was able to pass on many of the secrets of those earlier years.[11]

The techniques used by early decorators in producing a stenciled object are best illustrated by reproducing the top and front of the handsome bronze-stenciled New Portland box (Fig. 15 and Plate 9), from start to finish.[12] The stenciler began by creating or tracing an individual pattern. The latter required a tracing material of proper transparency.

For this purpose, he usually used tissue paper, which was coated with varnish, boiled linseed oil and turpentine, then thoroughly dried. From this he cut a piece of paper slightly larger than the element of the pattern being copied — which he placed over the pattern, holding it down with his free hand (Fig. 16).

With a soft lead pencil or fine pen and black ink, he traced the pattern carefully (Fig. 17). This process would be repeated for each element of the overall design. In this case, there would have been nine individual tracings in all.

These patterns were then transferred to stencil paper. To make good stencil paper for bronze stenciling, the old masters mixed equal parts of varnish, boiled linseed oil and turpentine in a container. After being shaken vigorously, the liquid was brushed on sheets of paper which had been removed from old account books. The coated paper was hung in the sun or some warm place to dry. These sheets of paper at times required a second coat of the mixture to obtain the desired transparency and flexibility.

There were two different ways to transfer the pattern onto the stencil. Often the stencil paper was transparent enough to place over the tracing. If so, by using a fine pen and black ink, the decorator retraced the pattern onto the stencil paper. A second way was to rub chalk on the bottom of the tracing, then place the tracing on stencil paper — and with a medium-hard lead — make an imprint. He also tried to leave one or more inches of paper beyond the cut points or edges of the stencil pattern (Fig. 18).

Figure 15:

Figure 16:

Figure 17:

Cutting the stencil from stencil paper was achieved by placing the paper on a piece of thick glass or some other hard, smooth, surface and cutting out the pattern with a sharply pointed, thin steel blade — which had to be sharpened often. If the decorator was right handed, the left hand controlled the paper; if he was left handed, the reverse was true (Fig. 19).

Next came the bronzing process. The painter needed two different bronze powders for the New Portland box: a fine, pale-gold powder and a fine silver (aluminum) powder. Decorators often used a palette for bronze powders which was made of a short nap velvet, measuring about ten by sixteen inches. They also cut several squares of short nap velvet, five inches square; these, held around the index finger, became the bronze powder applicators. In order to keep the material from raveling, it was necessary to either glue and trim the edges, or to turn the edges and stitch them down.

The surface of the piece was then given an evenly-spread coat of varnish over the red-black grained painted surface. This was allowed to dry to the point of slight tackiness when the varnish was touched. The decorator placed a small amount of each bronze on the bronzing palette; and then, with a ruler, determined the placement of the stencil and laid the stencil in place on the varnished surface. He wrapped a square of velvet around the index finger, dipped the wrapped finger gently into the bronze powder, and then tapped on the back of the other hand to remove any loose powder. After that, he started dusting the bronze powder through the stencil (Fig. 20), and continued in the same manner with all the stencils, until the duplication of Fig. 15 was achieved. This was left to dry for twenty-four hours, at which time the surface was wiped with a damp sponge to remove excess bronze powder. When again dry, the piece was given one or two coats of varnish. The product was a most attractive box; yet one which would have been eminently affordable.

Note: For further study on stenciling, consult the appropriate references in the bibliography.

Figure 18:

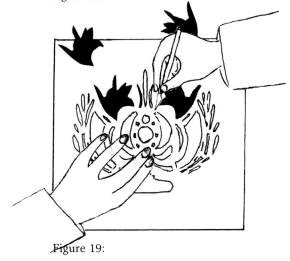

Figure 19:

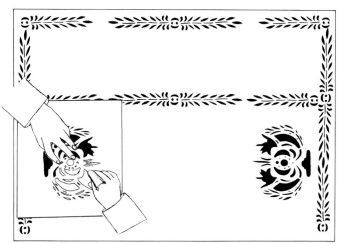

Figure 20:

Appendix A.

IDENTIFYING THE WOOD

In preparing this catalogue, a number of the pieces of furniture were examined in some detail to determine the types of woods used by the cabinetmakers. Given a block of wood, most woodworkers can tell by the grain, weight, and workability, what species they are holding. Once a piece of furniture has been assembled the wood may not be as easy to identify without defacing the object. Painted furniture offers a special challenge. The decorated surfaces of the pieces included in this exhibit are frequently covered by several layers of paint and varnish, completely obscuring the textural and visual characteristics of the wood.

With the gross characteristics well hidden, the elements of furniture selected for analysis were chosen carefully. Loose joints were dismantled so that the unpainted surfaces were accessible. Micro-examination techniques were the predominant type used. Small samples of wood were removed with a razor blade and where possible the three planes of wood structure were prepared: the transverse or cross section of the end grain; the radial or section parallel to the grain from the center of the tree to the bark; and the tangential or section parallel to the grain perpendicular to the radial section. Each sample was made by removing a shaving of sound wood less than 1/8" × 1/8" × 1/64". This was mounted in a glycerine, alcohol, and water solution on a glass micro-scope slide and examined with transmitted light at low (35×), medium (75×), and high (400×) magnifications with a standard compound microscope.

Under magnification there are a large number of varying structural elements of wood. With the use of "keys" published in standard wood science books,[1] most common woods can be readily separated. There are some woods that are quite difficult to differentiate without taking many samples (i.e., white and European birches from other American birches or hard maples from soft maples), while other woods that have very similar gross characteristics are readily distinguishable under the magnification of a compound microscope (i.e., maple from birch). For the purpose of this study, it was felt that the number of samples required for the separation of birch types and maple types would be too destructive. All of the 125+ wood samples that were examined turned out to be among a small number of the 113 types of wood that are native to Maine.[2]

Stephen W. Brooke
Conservator
Maine State Museum

Notes

I-A: The Woods and the Construction

1. [Augusta] *Kennebec Journal (KJ)*, 3/6/1829, 11/25/1831 and 4/29/1833; [Belfast] *Hancock Gazette and Penobscot Patriot (HGPP)*, 9/26/1821; [Gardiner] *Christian Intelligencer and Eastern Chronicle (CIEC)*, 6/6/1833.

2. *KJ*, 4/29/1833, 12/31/1841; *HGPP*, 2/22/1826; *Bangor Register (BR)*, 12/28/1826.

3. [Saco] *Maine Palladium (MP)*, 1/17/1827.

4. Nathaniel Knowlton Day Book, 1812-1859 [Eliot], MSS (Maine Historial Society, Portland, Maine); David Knowlton Day Book, 1826-1835 [Augusta], MSS (photocopy, Maine State Museum, Augusta, Maine); John Brewer Day Book, 1835-37 [Brewer], MSS (Old Sturbridge Village, Sturbridge, Massachusetts).

5. The wide spread in the per-foot cost of mahogany derives from the fact that the 12.5¢ per-foot price was for common boards, while that costing 75¢ per foot was called "branch mahogany," that is, figured wood. (David Knowlton Day Book, 2/27/1827 and 5/13/1828).

6. John Brewer Day Book, 1/24/1835, 3/19/1835, 5/8/1835, 5/16/1835, 1/28/1836, 6/4/1836, 7/25/1836, *passim*.

7. "Corey's Furniture Manufactory," *Portland Transcript (PT)*, 4/27/1850.

8. "Labor Saving Machinery and Increase of Manufacturing [at] A. & E. Dole Furniture Manufactory," *Bangor Daily Whig and Courier (BDWC)*, 7/7/1843.

9. *KJ*, 8/17/1832, 12/27/1844; *Lewiston Falls Journal (LFJ)*, 6/17/1848.

10. "Chests" in the account books refer to the form presently known as blanket chests and did include those with drawers. (For example, on 5/20/1815 Nathaniel Knowlton of Eliot made draw[er]s "for David Neal's chest.")

11. Bath maker's daybook, 1799-1805 [Bath, Maine], MSS (Maine State Museum, Augusta, Maine).

I-B: The Decoration

1. Dean A. Fales, Jr., *American Painted Furniture, 1660-1880* (New York: E. P. Dutton and Company, Inc., 1972), pp. 32-33, 70-71, 79.

2. Fales, *American Painted Furniture*, pp. 216-17.

3. *Ibid.*, p. 149.

4. *Maine Register, 1873-74*, pp. 104, 106, 115-16.

5. Morrill's Auctions, Inc., *Early American Country Antiques at Public Auction* [*Christopher Huntington collection*] (Portland: Portland Lithograph Co., 1974), p. 27; Samuel Pennington, "Guptill Family Estate Auction," *Maine Antiques Digest* (October, 1982), 1B - 2B; Charles Warren Spalding, *The Spalding Memorial: A Genealogical History of Edward Spalding of Virginia and Massachusetts Bay, and his Descendants* (Chicago: American Publication Association, 1897), p. 780; Federal Census: 1850 (Maine) (FC, 1850: Me.), r. 268, p. 166.

6. *HGPP*, May 30, 1821; *Belfast Gazette (BG)*, 10/23/1827; [Belfast] *Republican Journal (RJ)* 5/20/1839, 1/1/1845; 1847 Broadside by Howard and Town (photocopy at MSM); FC, 1850: Me., r. 270, pp. 137, 139; Federal Industrial Census: 1850 (Maine), MSS (at the Maine State Archives, Augusta, Maine) (FIC), p. 209, no. 21; Joseph Williamson, *History of the City of Belfast*, 2 vols. (Portland: Loring, Short, and Harmon, 1877), I, 725.

7. The process of coloring a plain surface with smoke from a candle (smoke decoration), is not really graining in the standard sense. However, because of the wide-spread use of the term "smoke-graining," it has been employed here.

8. Fales, *American Painted Furniture*, pp. 59-60; Charles F. Montgomery, *American Furniture: The Federal Period* (New York: Viking Press, 1966), p. 445; Gertrude Z. Thomas, "Lacquer: Chinese, Indian, 'Right' Japan and American," *Antiques* (June, 1961), 572-75.

9. Fales, *American Painted Furniture*, pp. 93-94, 133; Montgomery, *American Furniture: The Federal Period*, p. 446.

10. For examples, see: George Hepplewhite, *The Cabinet-Maker and Upholsterer's Guide*, 3rd. ed. (London: I. & J. Taylor, 1794; reprinted by Dover Publications, New York, 1969), plates 12, 13, 58, 78; and Thomas Sheraton, *The Cabinet-Maker and Upholsterer's Drawing Book*, 3rd ed. (London: T. Bensley, 1802; reprinted by Praeger Publishers, New York, 1970), plates 4, 16, 49.

11. Hepplewhite, *Cabinet-Maker and Upholsterer's Guide*, p. 2.

12. Sheraton, *Cabinet-Maker and Upholsterer's Drawing Book*, pp. 18, 19, 21; Thomas Sheraton, *The Cabinet Dictionary*, 2 vols. (London: W. Smith, 1803; reprinted by Praeger Publishers, New York, 1970), II, 415-34.

13. Earle G. Shettleworth, Jr., "The Radford Brothers: Portland Cabinet-makers of the Federal Period," *Antiques* (August, 1974), 285-287.

14. Sheraton, *Cabinet Dictionary*, II, 426-27.

15. Fales, *American Painted Furniture*, p. 179; Montgomery, *American Furniture: Federal Period*, pp. 163-65; Jane C. Giffen, "Susanna Rowson and Her Academy," *Antiques* (September, 1970), 436-440.

16. *Hallowell Gazette (HG)*, 3/8/1820

17. At this point, not much is known about the Bath Female Academy. It was incorporated in 1805 and a permanent building was constructed in 1825. Between those dates there were several Academy-related land transactions between the Academy proprietors. Probably the school was established in a rented space or a home during the early years. Ruth Arline Wray, *The History of Secondary Education in Cumberland and Sagadahoc Counties* (Orono, Maine: University Press, 1940), pp. 25, 34-35; Ava Harriet Chadbourne, *A History of Education in Maine* (Orono, Maine: [University Press], 1936), p. 113; [Portland], *Eastern Argus (EA)*, 10/7/1813.

18. Montgomery, *American Furniture: Federal Period*, pp. 462-63; Wendy A. Cooper, *In Praise of America: American Decorative Arts, 1650-1830* (New York: Knopf, 1980), pp. 116-17, 125; John T. Kenney, *The Hitchcock Chair* (New York: Clarkson N. Potter, Inc., 1971), pp. 70-71.

19. Fales, *American Painted Furniture*, pp. 178-79; Montgomery *American Furniture: Federal Period*, p. 463.

20. Fales, *American Painted Furniture*, pp. 224-225; personal communication from Katharine B. Hagler, Curator, Furniture, Henry Ford Museum, March 6, 1980.

21. Jean Lipman, *Rufus Porter: Yankee Pioneer* (New York: Clarkson N. Potter, Inc., 1968), pp. 89-170.

22. Esther Stevens Frazer, "The Golden Age of Stencilling," *Antiques* (April, 1922), 162-63; Esther Stevens Frazer, "Painted Furniture in America: The Sheraton Fancy Chair, 1790-1817," *Antiques* (June, 1924), 302-306; Fales, *American Painted Furniture*, pp. 132-147.

23. *EA*, 9/8/1803.

24. [Bath] *Maine Enquirer and Lincoln County Advertiser (MELCA)*, 1/4/1833; *RJ*, 9/1/1836; *KJ*, 5/29/1833; *BR*, 11/18/1828.

25. Fales, *American Painted Furniture*, pp. 95, 98, 105; Zilla Rides Lea, ed., *The Ornamental Chair: Its Development in America, 1700-1890* (Rutland, Vermont: Charles E. Tuttle Company, 1960), p. 116.

26. Sheraton, *Cabinet Dictionary*, II, 425.

27. Esther Stevens Frazer, "Painted Furniture in America: II: The Period of Stencilling, 1817-1835," *Antiques* (September, 1924), 141-46; Fales, *American Painted Furniture*, pp. 184-95; Kenney, *The Hitchcock Chair*, Chapters 4-7.

28. The inset turned balls on back spindles appear with regularity on documented or provenanced seating furniture from central and west central Maine. It is not a characteristic unique to the region (there are documented chairs with such inset balls from Rochester and Concord, New Hampshire [see *Plain and Elegant, Rich and Common: Documented New Hampshire Furniture, 1750-1850* (Concord: New Hampshire Historical Society, 1979), pp. 45, 138] and other examples, usually half-spindle, have been noted in eastern Massachusetts [personal communication with Nancy Goyne Evans, registrar, Winterthur Museum, 2/3/1983]) but it is well represented in the area.

29. Lea, *Ornamental Chair*, p. 82; Janet Waring, *Early American Stencils on Walls and Furniture* (New York: Dover Publications, Inc., 1968; reprint of 1937 publication by William R. Scott), p. 92. Waring felt that ormolu was the major inspiration for stenciled decorative motifs.

30. Thus far, with the exception of two boxes with Biddeford labels, all signed or provenanced pieces combining red and black graining with yellow striping and green banding have come from central interior Maine. As of this time, I am not aware of a documented item with this pattern from outside of Maine.

31. This data was compiled from the 1850 Maine Industrial Census and is on file at the Maine State Museum.

32. Interestingly, a contemporary of Stewart, John White of Woodstock, Vt. also looked to motifs found on painted tinware when decorating many of his chairs. Lea, *Ornamental Chair*, pp, 68-69, 72; N. Grier Parker, "John White, Chairmaker and Decorator," *The Decorator*, VI, No. 1 (1952), 15-16.

33. Personal correspondence with Dean McCrillis, Roxbury, Maine, February 7, 1983.

34. For the following three paragraphs the information on religion in Maine comes from Stephen Marini, "Religion in Maine, 1783-1820," paper presented at Maine and Statehood: A Symposium for Scholars sponsored by the Maine Humanities Council, Portland, Maine, December 3, 1982; Stephen Marini, *Radical Sects of Revolutionary New England* (Cambridge: Harvard University Press, 1982), chapters 3-5; "Memoir and Journals of Rev. Paul Coffin, D.D. of Buxton, Me.," Maine Historical Society, *Collections*, IV (1856), pp. 346-47, 388, 397. A graphic description of a camp meeting is given in "The Diary of Reverend Joseph Field: A Missionary Tour of the District of Maine [1805]," MSS, Kennebec Historical Society, July 3, 1805. Basic data on politics can be found in Ronald F. Banks, *Maine Becomes A State: The Movement to Separate Maine From Massachusetts, 1785-1820* (Middletown, Connecticut: Wesleyan University Press, 1970), pp. 83-87.

II: The Decorators

1. FC, 1850: Me, r. 252, p. 239 and r. 256, p. 11; *PD* 1850-51, p. 151 and *Bangor Directory (BD)* 1851, p. 19.

2. *HG*, 1/30/1822.

3. [Thomaston] *Lime Rock Gazette [LRG]*, 1/7/1846.

4. *Ellsworth American [Ells. Am.]*, 6/20/1856.

5. *HGPP*, 7/2/1823.

6. [Augusta] *Maine Patriot and State Gazette [MPSG]*, 4/27/1831.

7. [Bangor] *Penobscot Journal [PJ]*, 2/27/1832.

8. *Portland Gazette [PG]*, 11/16/1819.

9. *HG*, 1/30/1822.

10. [Ellsworth] *The Radical [TR]*, 7/17/1835; *MP*, 8/16/1826; *HG*, 4/13/1814; *BR*, 4/20/1826.

11. See checklist for John B. Hudson.

12. Information on Jepheth and Oliver Salem Beale comes from the *Vital Records of Bridgewater, Massachusetts to the Year 1850*, 2 vols. (Boston: New England Historical Genealogical Society, 1916). The connections between Horatio and the other two men are noted in the text.

13. Kennebec County Registry of Deeds (KCRD): 50, 176; and 63, 292.

14. KCRD: 52, 215.

15. *BR*, 5/5/1825. Somewhat confusing is a deed dated March 20, 1826, which still lists Horatio Beale as a resident of Augusta (KCRD: 56, 120).

16. *BR*, 4/20/1826, 12/28/1826, 12/10/1827, 4/22/1828, 11/4/1828.

17. *BR*, 1/20/1829, 6/30/1829; KCRD: 67, 378; *BD* 1834.

18. KCRD: 63, 98; 112, 551.

19. *Vital Records of Bridgewater*, I, 47; Edwin A. Churchill, et al., *Landmark of Service: Chapters in the History of Methodism in Augusta, 1828-1978* (Augusta, Maine: The Green Street United Methodist Church, 1978), pp. 4-5; James W. North, *The History of Augusta* (Augusta, Maine: Clapp and North, 1870), pp. 486-87; Obituary (of Jepheth Beale), *KJ*, 2/27/1867.

20. KCRD: 7, 429; 23, 282; 16, 346.

21. KCRD: 32, 143; 75, 379; 83, 214; 40, 289.

22. KCRD: 108, 509; 107, 334; 111, 318; Churchill, *Landmark of Service*, p. 4.

23. KCRD: 136, 396; 152, 37; 200, 67; FC, 1850: Me., r. 256, p. 20. Ethel Colby Conant, ed., *Vital Records of Augusta, Maine to the Year 1892* (Portland, Maine: Maine Historical Society, 1934), p. 233.

24. FC, 1850: Me., r. 256, p. 20.

25. *KJ*, 2/20/1846.

26. *KJ*, 3/24/1848.

27. KCRD: 182, 504; 195, 250; 210, 333.

28. KCRD: 32, 143; Ronald Vern Jackson, Gary Ronald Teeples, David Schaefermeyer, eds., *Maine, 1810 Census Index* (Bountiful, Utah; Accelerated Indexing Systems, 1976); Churchill, *Landmark of Service*, p. 4.

29. *KJ*, VI, 9/24/1829.

30. *MPSG*, 11/17/1830.

31. *Augusta Courier [AC]*, 8/10/1832.

32. *BD* 1843, 1846, 1848, 1851.

33. KCRD: 145, 108; 200, 67; 182, 504; 210, 333; 162, 100; 178, 551.

34. Daniel Knowlton's Daybook, 4/10/1830, 4/27/1830; 10/14/1831, etc.

35. Churchill, *Landmark of Service*, p. 4; North, *History of Augusta*, pp. 486-89.

36. Churchill, *Landmark of Service*, pp. 4-5, 15; North, *History of Augusta*, pp. 487-88.

37. KCRD: 63, 297.

38. [Portland] *Jeffersonian, [JJ]*, 9/7/1835.

39. Charles Albert Hayden, comp. (revised by Jessie Hale Tuttle), *The Capen Family: Descendants of Bernard Capen of Dorchester, Mass.* (Minneapolis: Augsburg Publishing House, 1929), p. 138; *PD* 1823; *EA*, 10/31/1824.

40. *Constitution and History of the Maine Charitable Mechanics Association* (Portland: Published by the Association, 1965), p. 81; Hayden, *Capen*, p. 208.

41. *Portland Advertiser [PA]*, 7/29/1827.

42. *PA*, 10/4/1859. Capen is listed as a sign painter in the 1834, 1837, 1841, 1844, 1846, 1847-8, 1856, 1858-9, and 1863-4 *Portland Directories*.

43. *PA*, 10/4/1859; *PT*, 3/28/1863.

44. Cited in Michael McCann, *Artist Beware* (New York: Watson-Guptill Publications, 1979), p. 2.

45. McCann, *Artist Beware*, p. 215.

46. Charles Henry Wright Stocking, *The History and Genealogy of the Knowltons of England and America* (New York: The Knickerbocker Press, 1897), p. 148.

47. Nathaniel Knowlton Account Book, 8/10/1812 - 11/15/1814; William J. Lamson, *Descendants of William Lamson of Ipswich, Mass., 1634-1917* (New York: Tobias A. Wright, 1917), p. 127.

48. See for examples: Nathaniel Knowlton Account Book, 3/28/1815, and 7/26/1815, 2/28/1824, 9/17/1824, 5/23/1827, 12/23/1827, and 4/7/1830.

49. *Ibid.*, 8/21/1822, 5/21/1829, 6/9/1831.

50. *Ibid.*, 8/8/1815, 4/10/1816, 8/11/1817, *passim*.

51. *Ibid.*, 2/13/1823, 3/7/1823, 9/4/1823, 3/1/1832, 3/19/1835, and 4/5/1849.

52. *Ibid.*, 1/3/1815, 2/14/1822, and 8/6/1824.

53. *Ibid.*, 3/16/1818, 10/16/1818, 3/10/1832, and 7/11/1833.

54. *Ibid.*, 8/1/1818, 5/24/1821, 1/18/1823.

55. *Ibid.*, 9/6/1824.

56. *Ibid.*, 6/30/1832.

57. *Ibid.*, 6/12/1821, 11/24/1832, 9/27/1833, 6/10/1834, 6/9/1842, *passim*.

58. *Ibid.*, Vol. II; FC, 1850: Me., r. 274, p. 255.

59. FC, 1850: Me., r. 274, p. 255; Stocking, *Knowlton*, pp. 148, 382-83.

60. *BR*, 3/17/1825.

61. *BR*, 7/7/1825, 4/13/1826, 12/24/1828.

62. *BR*, 6/29/1826, 12/21/1826.

63. *BR*, 4/11/1827.

64. *BR*, 1/16/1828.

65. *BR*, 3/25/1828.

66. *BR*, 11/17/1829.

67. Ronald Vern Jackson and Gary Ronald Teeples, eds., *Maine, 1830 Census Index* (Bountiful, Utah: Accelerated Indexing Systems, Inc., 1977).

68. Data on individuals contained in checklist.

69. Waring, *Early American Stencils*, pp. 133-35; *PD* 1846, 1847-8.

70. Waring, *Early American Stencils*, p. 134.

III-B: History and Execution of Bronze Stenciling

1. G. Koizumi, *Lacquer Work* (London: Sir Isaac Pitman and Sons, Ltd., 1923), p. 14.

2. *Ibid.*, p. 17; W.D. John and Anne Simcox, *Pontypool and Usk-Japanned Wares* (Bath, England; Harding and Curtis, Ltd., 1953), p. 3.

3. John and Simcox, p. 31.

4. *Ibid.*, p. 30.

5. Lea, *Ornamented Tray*, p. 163; Waring, *Early American Stencils*, p. 102.

6. Lea, *Ornamented Tray*, p. 135; Maria D. Murry, *The Art of Tray Painting* (New York: Bramhall House, 1954), p. 58.

7. Dard Hunter, *Paper Making* (New York: Dover Publications, Inc., 1943), pp. 468-70, 472, 474; Waring, *Early American Stencils*, pp. 6-8.

8. Waring, *Early American Stencils*, pp. 89-91.

9. *Ibid.*, pp. 92-99, 105-111.

10. *Ibid.*, pp. 100, 113, 116, 121, 123; Kenney, *Hitchcock Chair*, p. 77.

11. Waring, *Early American Stencils*, p. 133; Kenney, *Hitchcock Chair*, p. 78.

12. An excellent contemporary description of stenciling (called "Bronze Gilding") can be found in *The Mechanics Assistant, Being a Select Collection of Valuable Receipts* (Utica, New York: D. Bennett & Co., 1830), pp. 21-22.

Appendix A

1. *Forest Trees of Maine*, Bulletin 24, Maine Forestry Department (Augusta, Me., 1973).

2. A.J. Panshin and Carl de Zeeuw, *Textbook of Wood Technology* (New York: McGraw-Hill, 1970).

Lombard Sheraton Chamber Table

Extensive painted decoration. Vining leaves spiraling around legs. Foliate sprays bordering edges. Poems entitled "Hope" and "Continued" inscribed on table top, flanking a basket of fruit, grapes, leaves and tendrils. Shell arrangement with seaweed in four corners of top with floral design bordering outside edge. Townscapes painted on sides. Drawer front has decorator's name painted in fancy script above a small basket of fruit and surrounded by flowers and birds.

Dimensions: H. 33″ W. 31″ D. 16″
Materials: maple
Date: 1816
Marks: painted across drawer front, "Elizabeth Paine Lombard Feb 1816"
Collection of the Shelburne Museum, Shelburne, Vt., 3.6-61
History: The table was painted by Elizabeth Paine Lombard of Bath, Me. It is probable that Elizabeth Lombard studied decorative painting at the Bath Female Academy.
Sources: Cooper, *In Praise of America,* pp. 116-117, 125
Kenney, *Hitchcock Chair,* pp. 70-71

Country Sheraton Stand

Extensive painted decoration on unpainted wood. Vining leaves spiraling around legs. Foliate sprays bordering top edge. Basket of fruit on top. Poems inscribed on drawer front and back of table. Houses and trees painted on sides. Brass pull.

Dimensions: H. 28½'' W. 16¼'' D. 18¼''
Materials: case, top and legs, maple; drawer interior, pine; pull, brass
Date: c. 1815-1830
Marks: written in ink script on inside bottom of drawer, "Table purchased from Lawrence Kinney of Farmington, Maine. Table purchased by him from a farm at Kents Hill, Maine. E. Martin, M.D. Sold to George Morrill of Harrison, Maine. E.M."
Collection of George Morrill, Harrison, Me.
History: Found in Kents Hill, this table has been painted in a manner that seems essentially a folk art interpretation of the Academy art tradition. Interestingly, the scenes on the sides are very similar to the Rufus Porter school of mural art.
Source: Lipman, *Rufus Porter: Yankee Pioneer,* pp. 89-158

Carney Country Hepplewhite Stand

Base of stand and legs painted yellow. Smoke-grained top. Black striping on edges and olive green band running length of legs and outlining drawer and top. Drawer has stamped brass rosette pulls, but back plates are missing.

Dimensions: H. 28″ W. 21″ D. 15½″
Materials: white pine; pulls, brass
Date: c. 1820-1840
MSM 82.15.1
History: This stand came from the Carney homestead in Sheepscot, Me. Franklin L. Carney established himself at the spot in the early nineteenth century. His daughter married Arthur L. Doe, who took over the property; the house still remains in the hands of Doe family descendants.

Plate no. 4

Tuck Country Sheraton Dressing Table

Painted yellow with black striping and trim. Silver stencil of fruit motif on center of both drawers and bordered by green freehand painted leaves. Silver stencil of leaves outlining drawer tops. Brass pulls on drawers.

Dimensions: H. 38" W. 33" D. 17"
Materials: frame, top and drawer front, white pine; drawer interior and legs, basswood; drawer pulls, brass
Date: c. 1830-1840
Marks: printed paper labels, (1) on back, "MANUFACTURED BY MADISON TUCK, FOOT OF WINTHROP - STREET, - HALLOWELL, M.T. KEEPS CONSTANTLY ON HAND A GOOD ASSORTMENT OF Cabinet Furniture and Chairs." (2) on lower drawer bottom, "MADISON TUCK, CABINET MAKER, HALLOWELL"
MSM 82.82.1 Donated by Maine Antiques Digest, Waldoboro, Me.
History: Madison Tuck was born in Fayette, Me. on December 17, 1809. He settled in Hallowell about 1830 and married Mary A. Woodbridge of Hallowell on April 4, 1832. Tuck left his cabinetmaking business by 1840. Through the 1850s he pursued several other careers such as trader, butcher and yeoman. Actively involved in land trading, Tuck overextended himself by the late 1850s and suffered a series of foreclosures. Madison Tuck died on December 10, 1894.
Sources: FC, 1850: Me., r. 256, p. 201
KCRD: 77,210-211; 84,226; 120,422; 126,26; 138,537; 145,208; 199,468
AC: 12/1/1831

Readfield Country Sheraton Dressing Table

Drawer fronts grained to simulate mahogany. Sides of upper case and main stand grained to simulate bird's-eye maple. Tops of upper case and main stand, legs and backboard grained to simulate common maple. Stamped round brass pulls.

Dimensions: H. 45'' W. 35¼'' D. 19½''
Materials: all basswood, except for smaller upper drawer which is wholly white
                pine; pulls, brass
Date: c. 1830-1835
Marks: See History
MSM 74.45.6
History: The table has several political inscriptions on the bottom of the upper case
           drawer. All of the men mentioned, other than Andrew Jackson, were
           National Republicans. "Hunton Forever" refers to Jonathan Hunton of
           Readfield, Me. who served as Governor of Maine for 1829-1830. "Daniel
           Goodenow Forever" refers to Goodenow who ran unsuccessfully for
           governor in 1831, 1832 and 1833. "Clay Forever" and "Clayites in Read-
           field" refer to Henry Clay from Kentucky; Clay lost the presidential elec-
           tion to Andrew Jackson in 1832. "A Jackas" and "Few Jackson Jackasses
           [in Readfield]" refer to Andrew Jackson, President of the United States
           from 1829-1837. Jackson, a Democrat, was detested by the pro-Clay
           National Republicans, whose strength in Maine had grown in the 1820s.
Sources: *Maine Register, 1873-74,* pp. 104, 106, 115-116
           Morrill's Auction, Inc., *Early American Country Antiques at Auction,* p. 40,
           no. 301

Leighton Box

Ochre and brown graining with darker brown banding. Green painted oval in center of top.

Dimensions: H. 10¼'' W. 26¼'' D. 13''
Materials: basswood
Date: c. 1847
Marks: inscribed on back while paint was wet, "Esther Leighton, Augusta Maine
           December 1847"
MSM 82.17.2
History: Esther Leighton was the daughter of Augusta farmer Ephraim, Jr. and
           Hannah. She was fifteen years old when her name was inscribed on
           the box.
Source: FC, 1850: Me., r 256, p. 91

Williams Country Sheraton Dressing Table

Painted yellow with black and dark green banding and red striping outlining major elements. Red and green painted teardrop pattern on front legs and backboard. Free-hand black painted curlicues frame bronze stencil of fruit and leaf motif on backboard. Bronze rosette stencil on black painted scrolled ends of backboard. Black painted turned feet. Simulated bird's eye maple drawer fronts. Glass pulls of Deming Jarves, Boston and Sandwich, design.

Dimensions: H. 38½'' W. 36'' D. 16¾''
Materials: frame, top and drawer front, white pine; upper case and case drawers, main drawer interior and legs, basswood; drawer pulls, glass
Date: February, 1832
Marks: written in pencil on back boards, ''J. Williams, Feby, 1832''; ''John Williams''
Former collection of Mr. and Mrs. W. M. Schwind, Jr., Yarmouth, Me.
History: John Williams, the maker of this table, was born in Chesterville, Me. on January 6, 1801, the son of Captain Thomas and Lydia Williams. Thomas was a joiner by trade and a locally prominent individual; unfortunately he succumbed to alcohol, being put into town guardianship in 1808 and dying two years later. John, with two brothers and two sisters, helped his mother run the family farm until he reached his mid-twenties when he turned to cabinet making. In 1827, he moved to Mount Vernon, where he continued in the trade until 1885. Williams died on June 18, 1888 in Mount Vernon.

The glass knobs used by Williams on the drawers of this dressing table were manufactured under the 1829 patent to Deming Jarves of the Boston and Sandwich Glass Works, ''for pressing glass knobs and screws.'' Each knob terminates in a glass screw that turns into a threaded hole in the drawer front.
Sources: FC, 1850: Me., r. 257, p. 374
FIC, 1870: Me., Mt. Vernon
KCRD: 59,200; 62,469; 63,426
KCRP: W8; File 12, Docket 4982
Lilly and Hewing, [Chesterville] Town Records, p. 21
MBD, 1855, 1869, 1874-1875, 1880, 1885
Jackson, et. al., Maine 1830 Census List
''   ''   ''   ''   1840   ''   ''
Sewall, History of Chesterville
McKearin, Helen, ''The Case of the Pressed Glass Knobs,'' Antiques, LX (Augusta, 1951), p. 118-120
Personal communication with Arlene Palmer Schwind of Yarmouth, Me., April 16, 1983

Tobey Country Sheraton Dressing Table

Red and black graining in wide, generally horizontal striations across main elements, with daubed patterns on legs and yellow banding around drawer. Brass pull on drawer. Companion piece to washstand.

Dimensions: H. 34 7/8'' W. 31'' D. 15¾''
Materials: frame and drawer front, white pine; top, drawer and drawer interior, basswood; pull, brass
Date: c. 1825-1840
MSM 81.96.2
History: This piece belonged to Raymond W. Tobey. He was of the fourth generation of his family to live in Fairfield, Me., his ancestors having arrived during the late eighteenth century. The dressing table remained a part of the Tobey homestead until it was acquired by the Museum in the autumn of 1981.
Sources: Christine Brown, "Vital Records of Fairfield, Maine," typescript, 1980 (at Maine State Library), pp. 82, 188-190, 345-346, 552
(H.E.) Mitchell and Davis, comp., *The Fairfield Register, 1904,* (Kents Hill, Maine, 1904), pp. 8-9, 99

Tobey Country Sheraton Washstand

Red and black graining in wide, generally horizontal striation across main elements, with daubed patterns on legs and yellow banding around drawer. Brass pull on drawer. Companion piece to dressing table.

Dimensions: H. 39½'' W. 16½'' D. 15''
Materials: frame, drawer front and backboard, white pine; top, legs and drawer interior, basswood; pull, brass
Date: c. 1825-1840
MSM 81.121.1
History: See above

Hubbard Washstand

Painted yellow with light and dark olive banding, and black striping outlining major elements. Dark green leaves and brown fruit painted on center of backboard and drawer front, and enclosed in black curlicue design. Brown leaves painted on scrolled ends of backboard. Brass pull.

Dimensions: H. 34¼'' W. 16¼'' D. 14¾''
Materials: lower frame and drawer front, white pine; upper frame, top, drawer
　　　　　interior and legs, basswood; pull, brass
Date: c. 1830-1845
Collection of an anonymous lender
History: This washstand was found in the estate of Governor John Hubbard (1794-
　　　　　1869) of Hallowell. The Hubbard family home on Winthrop Street,
　　　　　together with many documented estate items including this washstand,
　　　　　descended in the Hubbard family until recent times.

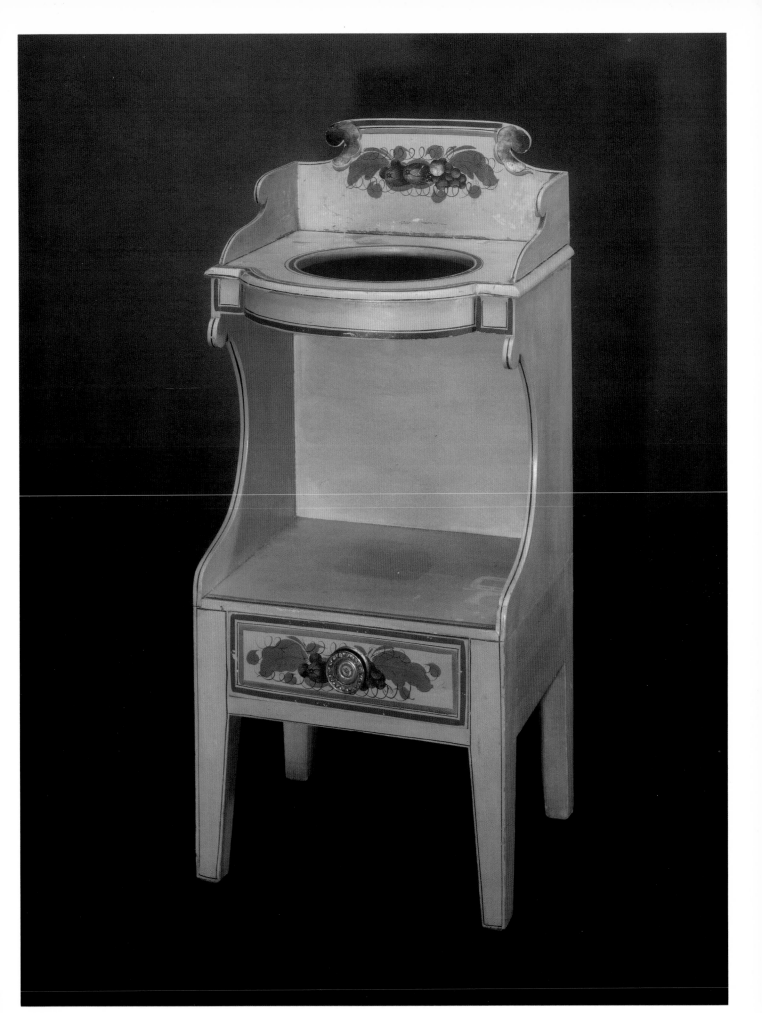

New Portland Two-Drawer Blanket Chest

Black on red graining with bronze stenciling on top and front. Stencil of stag and dog around edges of top. Stencil of basket around key holes on chest front. Exotic stencils also on the front. Stenciling pattern similar to the box below . Stamped brass pulls.

Dimensions: H. 36¼" W. 39½" D. 18"
Materials: case, top and backboards, white pine; drawer fronts, birch; drawer
            interiors, basswood; pulls, brass
Date: c. 1825-1840
Marks: inscribed in wet paint on top, "New Portland"
MSM 74.45.2
History: The chest, a piece from the Christopher Huntington collection, was
            acquired through auction.
Source: Morrill's Auction, Inc., *Early American Country Antiques at Auction*, p. 22,
            no. 162

New Portland Box

Black on red graining with bronze stenciling on front, sides and top. Stencils of flower, leaf, and small diamond motifs on the top. Stencils of wolf, rabbit and fox on the front. Stenciling patterns similar to the blanket chest above.

Dimensions: H. 11¼" W. 25¾" D. 13½"
Materials: basswood, except for white pine bottom
Date: c. 1825-1835
MSM 81.121.2
History: This box was acquired along the central Maine coast and was decorated
            by the same individual as the blanket chest above.

Tobey Two-Drawer Blanket Chest

Red and black banded graining. Top and front horizontally grained. Drawers grained diagonally. Sides grained vertically.

Dimensions: H. 38½'' W. 39¼'' D. 15¾''
Materials: case, drawer fronts and backboard, white pine; drawer interiors, basswood; legs, birch; drawer pulls, walnut
Date: c. 1830-1845
MSM 81.96.3
History: See Plate 7

Two-Drawer Blanket Chest

Ochre yellow, green and brown sponged graining.

Dimensions: H. 40'' W. 39½'' D. 18¾''
Materials: case, top, drawer fronts and backboards, white pine; drawer interiors,
　　　　basswood
Date: c. 1830-1839
Marks: inscribed in blue crayon on back, "A D 183[?]"; undecipherable words
　　　　in white chalk also on back
Collection of Roberta Hansen, Yarmouth, Me.
History: This chest was acquired from the Solon area, and is similar in decoration
　　　　to others from that area.

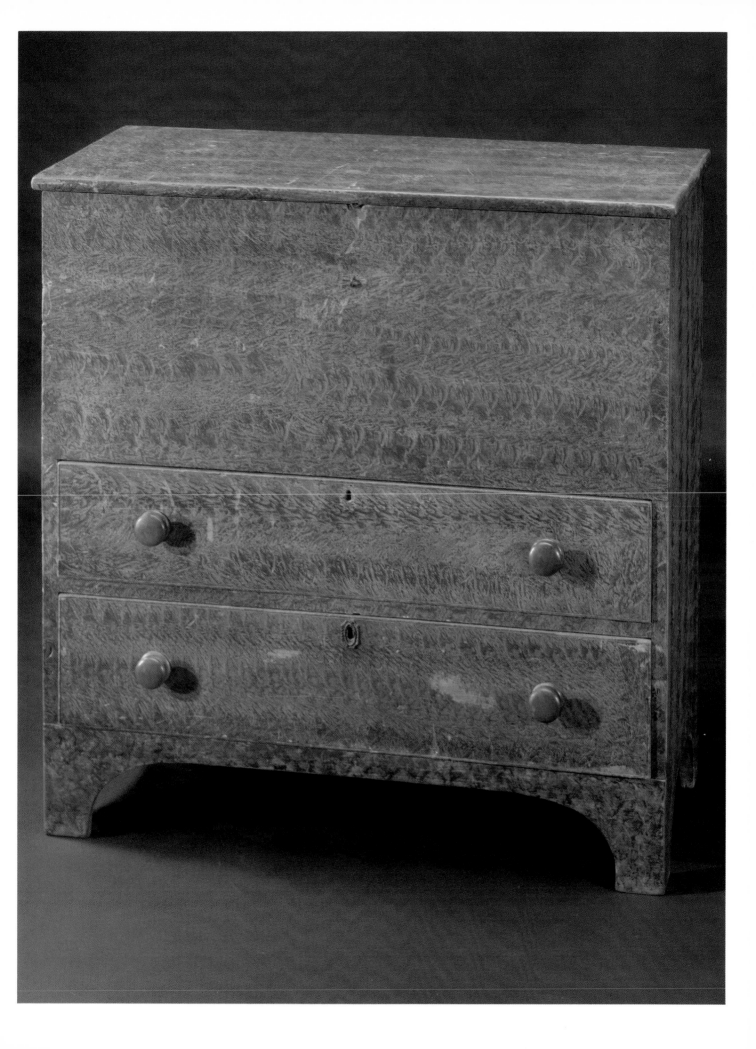

Merrill Empire Bureau

Red on black graining with yellow striping and green banding. Brass rosettes on backboard. Replacement brass pulls.

Dimensions: H. 45″ W. 44″ D. 22¼″
Materials: white pine except for beech legs; brass rosettes and pulls.
Date: c. 1825-1845
Marks: written in pencil in script on back, "C.H. Merrill, So. Paris"
MSM 82.13.1
History: The bureau was found in the Paris Hill area. Charles H. Merrill was the grandson of William Merrill, who established a South Paris farm in 1816. William and James, his son and Charles' father, were both farmers. Charles was born in 1860 and married a local girl, Rosa Sturtevant. However, by 1906, he was no longer a resident of South Paris, having died or moved.
Sources: William B. Lapham and Silas P. Maxim, *History of Paris, Maine*, (Paris, Maine: Printed for the authors, 1884), pp. 677-678, 741
Mitchell and Davis, comp., *The Paris Register, 1906*, (Brunswick, Me.: H.E. Mitchell, Co., 1906)

Empire Bureau

Painted yellow with red striping and green banding outlining major elements. Smoke-grained drawer fronts. Black vase-turned feet. Stamped brass pulls.

Dimensions: H. 49½'' W. 43½'' D. 20¼''
Materials: case and drawer fronts, white pine; drawer interiors, basswood;
       pulls, brass
Date: c. 1825-1845
Collection of Kenneth and Paulette Tuttle, Pittston, Me.
History: The bureau was acquired from Rumford Point, Me.

Desk-on-Frame

Reddish brown and yellow sponged graining. The frame is of later date than the desk proper.

Dimensions: H. 39½'' W. 26¾'' D. 18½''
Materials: probably pine
Date: c. 1820-1840
Marks: written with pencil in script on bottom side of lift top, ''Thomaston'', plus
      several undecipherable words
Collection of the William A. Farnsworth Museum, Rockland, Me.
History: The Thomaston desk-on-frame is part of the original furniture in the
      William A. Farnsworth Homestead in Rockland. William A. Farnsworth
      (1816-1876) was a native of Waldoboro who moved to East Thomaston
      (later Rockland) about 1840. He built and moved into the Homestead about
      1850, probably bringing the desk with him. The desk was used in the
      home, probably in the kitchen, as various graffiti by the Fransworth
      children will attest. The desk is signed on the inside of the top by its
      Thomaston maker; unfortunately, the signature is illegible.

Alexander Empire Desk

Black on red graining to simulate mahogany. Stamped brass pulls.

Dimensions: H. 44″ W. 40¼″ D. 28 3/8″ (open) D. 19½″ (closed)
Materials: drawer divider between top and second drawer, birch; legs, beech;
        remainder, white pine; pulls, brass
Date: c. 1830-1840
Marks: inscribed on drawer inside, "Lydia Alexander Hiram ME"
MSM 82.16.1
History: The secretary originally belonged to the Jonas Alexander family of Hiram,
        Me. Mr. Fred Stanton, an Alexander on his mother's side, gave it to Mrs.
        Wilbur R. Small of E. Hiram. As of yet Lydia's relationship to the family
        has not been determined.
Sources: FC, 1850: Me., r. 262, p. 87
        Personal correspondence with Mrs. Wilbur R. Small, East Hiram, Me.,
        December, 1981

Bourgoin Cupboard (Buffet)

Blue painted exterior. Mid-section molding replaced.

Dimensions: H. 84'' W. 46 1/8'' D. 21 7/8''
Materials: white pine
Date: c. 1840-1860
MSM 82.112.1
History: The cupboard was acquired in Madawaska, Me. Originally it had been in
       the Hector Bourgoin family, which was one of the first families to settle
       the Frenchville area.

Plate no. 17

Tall Case Clock

Sponged ochre and cream graining with red and yellow daubed decoration. Sponged in spiral graining on base and sides. White painted dial with gilt colored scrolled elements on corners and basket of multicolored flowers on top. Open worked hands.

Dimensions: H. 82¼″ W. 20″ D. 9¾″
Materials: white pine
Date: c. 1815-1835
Marks: painted on clock dial, ''R. Whiting''
Collection of Kenneth and Paulette Tuttle, Pittston, Me.
History: The clock was acquired from a house in Farmington, Me. The clock's workings were made by Riley Whiting of Winchester, Ct.

Deane Bed Headboard

Black on red graining with yellow banding outlining the scrolled headboard. Bronze stencils of leaves on balls of posts and bolsters

Dimensions: H. 51½'' W. 53¼''
Materials: posts, maple; headboard, white pine
Date: c. 1830-1840
MSM 77.13.1 Donated by the Maine State Organization, D.A.R.
History: The bed originally belonged to Stephan R. Deane of West Leeds, Me., who lived from 1816 to 1898. Stephan Deane taught school at Kents Hill, Leeds and in Massachusetts. He returned to Maine in 1852 where he became the West Leeds postmaster. From 1859 on, he served many terms on the school committee and wrote the history of the West Leeds schools when the Androscoggin County history was prepared. Stephan Deane also operated a calligraphy school. The bed was acquired from the family home.
Source: Communication from Marius Peladeau, Warren, Me., March 14, 1977 (MSM files)

Plate no. 19

Tobey Bed

Black and red graining with gilt striping on head and foot boards. Stenciled vining decorations around balls and bells of posts and bolsters. Large floral motif stencil on center of headboard. Large stencil of bowl with fruit and vines on center of footboard.

Dimensions: H. 46'' L. 77 5/8'' W. 55½''
Materials: posts, maple; headboard, basswood
Date: c. 1825-1840
MSM 81.102.2
History: See Plate 7

Box (top)

Black on red graining with yellow striping and freehand curlicues. Gilt stencils on lid, sides and front, including basket of fruit, basket of flowers and leaf motifs. Stencil of five pointed star inside of floral rosette is the same as that used on "D.G." box. Lock on top is missing.

Dimensions: H. 11¾'' W. 29¼'' D. 14½''
Materials: basswood
Date: c. 1830-1840
MSM 81.96.5
History: See above.

D.G. Box (bottom)

Black on red graining with yellow striping and bronze stenciling of fruit, flower and leaf motifs on top, front and sides. Initials "D.G." on top which are surrounded by freehand yellow curlicues. Stencil of five pointed star inside of floral rosette is the same as that used on box above.

Dimensions: H. 10¾'' W. 28¼'' D. 13¼''
Materials: basswood
Date: c. 1830-1840
Marks: inscribed on top, "D.G."
MSM 82.14.1
History: The box was decorated by the same individual as the box below.
        It was acquired from a Skowhegan, Me. home.

Box (top left)

Off-white (cream) and black graining. Band of black paint on edges. Back unpainted.

Dimensions: H. 9 3/16'' W. 20¾'' D. 10 1/8''
Materials: basswood
Date: c. 1815-1830
MSM 82.8.1
History: The box was acquired from a Skowhegan, Me. home

Weston Box (top right)

Salmon sponged graining. Blue-black feathered decoration on corners and outside edge of top.

Dimensions: H. 10½'' W. 30½'' D. 15''
Materials: basswood
Date: c. 1820-1840
MSM 71.131.19   Donated by the Benjamin Weston family heirs
History: The box was acquired from the Weston family homestead in Madison, Me.
       Benjamin Weston was one of Madison's first settlers, arriving in 1786.
       His father, Joseph, was the founder of Skowhegan. The family farmstead
       was built in 1817 and is still owned by family members.

Carter Box (bottom)

Black on red graining. Yellow painted ovals daubed with red and black paint and randomly placed on front and sides.

Dimensions: H. 12¼'' W. 29¾'' D. 16''
Materials: white pine
Date: c. 1830-1845
Marks: inscribed in paint on top while still wet, "James M Carter, Rumford,
       Maine"; penciled in script on inside of top, "Amasa Carter"
MSM 78.98.1
History: James M. Carter was born on March 2, 1815 in Rumford, Me., the son of
       Ephraim and Hannah. In the 1850 census, James Carter was listed as a
       farmer. He and his wife, Martha, had two children, Mary (born c. 1846)
       and Amasa (born c. 1848)
Source: FC, 1850: Me., r. 262, p. 218

Box (top)

Green painted with red and black striping and yellow banding. Acorns and stylized yellow leaves with red veining painted on top front border. Red pinwheel and basket designs appear on front and top. Large red balls painted on four corners of sides. Back painted blue/green.

Dimensions: H. 10¾" W. 24" D. 12"
Materials: probably pine
Date: c. 1835
Marks: painted on back, "Jn x C.y x 1835"
Collection of Kenneth and Paulette Tuttle, Pittston, Me.
History: The box was acquired from a home in Augusta, Me. Local broadsides
         and newspapers dating 1834 and 1835 line the box's interior.

Box (bottom)

Painted olive green with dark yellow borders containing white stamped diamonds on front, sides and top. Back painted olive green but has no design. Base molding painted dark green with a design of leaves and berries in mustard and dark red colors, and appears to be freehand. Top molding of base is dark blue.

Dimensions: H. 7 7/8" W. 19" D. 8 7/8"
Materials: tupelo
Date: c. 1815-1830
MSM 82.7.1
History: The box is decorated with a stamped diamond pattern which has been
         found on a pair of chairs with a strong family history to Livermore, Me.
Source: Personal correspondence from Dean McCrillis, Roxbory, Me., February 7,
         1983

Stewart Step-Down Windsor Side Chair

Salmon colored background with red and green painted decoration. Red striping outlining major elements. Green band outlining seat front. Green and red teardrops on legs and spindles. Green ball with black and red stripes, and green and red ferns on crest rail.

Dimensions: H. 35¾" SW. 16¼" SD. 15¾"
Materials: seat, probably basswood
Date: c. 1812-1827
Marks: paper label on seat bottom, "DANIEL STEWART, Chair-Maker & Painter, Farmington, ME."
Collection of Burton and Helaine Fendelman, New York
History: Daniel Stewart was born in Martha's Vineyard, Mass. on August 30, 1786. He moved with his family to Farmington, Me. in 1794 where his father, Hugh, carried on the trades of housewright and chairmaker. Daniel took up the chairmaking and painting trade and produced some of the most handsome Windsors documented to a Maine maker. Unfortunately, he died in 1827, at only 41 years of age.
Sources: KCRP: S15
Butler, *History of Farmington,* pp. 576-578
Santore, *Windsor Style in America,* p. 51

Country Hepplewhite Stand

Red and black graining with yellow striping and green banding on drawer, top, sides and legs.

Dimensions: H. 28½'' W. 22'' D. 19¾''
Materials: frame, top, drawer front and bottom, white pine; drawer sides and back, basswood
Date: c. 1825-1840
Collection of Kenneth and Paulette Tuttle, Pittston, Me.
History: The stand was acquired from a home in Mechanic Falls, Me.

Weymouth Thumb-back Windsor Side Chair (set of four)

Red and black grained with yellow striping and green bands. Rose and foliage bronze stencils.

Dimensions: H. 32 5/8'' W. 16½'' D. 17''
Materials: seat, white pine; back posts, maple; spindles, poplar (aspen); legs, beech; stretchers, birch
Date: c. 1825-1840
Marks: written on seat bottom in pencil, ''E Weymouth''
MSM 81.2.2-5
History: The set of chairs was found in Maine about three years ago. It is probable that E. Weymouth was the owner, and although nothing definite has yet been developed, this individual might have been Ebenezer Weymouth, a stone mason from Saco or Elbridge Weymouth, a farmer from Wales.
Sources: FC, 1850: Me., r. 257, p. 52 and r. 275, p. 319

White Thumb-back Windsor Side Chair (left)

Black on red graining with green banding and yellow striping on major elements. Stylized geometric shapes with centered spoked wheel stenciled on crest rail. Stencil badly worn.

Dimensions: H. 33″ W. 17″ D. 18½″
Materials: not tested; however two similar White chairs were microscopically analyzed and both had basswood seats and all other elements made of birch.
Date: c. 1836-1840
Marks: printed paper label on seat bottom, "Samuel K. White, Fairfield, ME.";
"Fairfield" has been crossed out and replaced by "Dexter," written in ink
Collection of Charles and Nancy Burden, Woolwich, Me.
History: Samuel Kilburn White was born in Sterling, Mass. on October 17, 1798. He was in Fairfield, Me., constructing chairs by the early 1820s. After a decade, he began moving around: Old Town, 1834-36; Dexter, 1837-39; and Exeter, 1841-49. He died in Exeter in 1849 at the age of fifty-one.
Sources: FC, 1850: Me., Vol 27, Sched. 3, No. 19
White, *Genealogy of the Descendants of John White*, II, 203

Late Fancy Vase-back Side Chair (right)

Red and black graining. Yellow striping on seat, legs and stretchers. Bronze stencils of a landscape on crest rail, a temple on vase-back, and geometric shapes on back posts. Back of seat, crest rail and vase-back daubed black on red.

Dimensions: H. 32½″ W. 17″ D. 15″
Materials: seat, softwood; back post, birch; crest rail and legs, maple
Date: c. 1825-1850
Marks: painted in black on bottom of seat, "JCT"
MSM 78.21.63 Donated by Miss Carrie D. Files of Cumberland Center, Me.
History: The chair descended through the Snow family of Thorndike, Me.

Plate no. 26

Corey Hitchcock Type Side Chair (left)

Black base coat with gold striping outlining major elements. Bronze stencil of rosette motif on turned crest rail. Bronze stencil of basket of fruit and leaf motif on back splat. Bronze stencil of flower and leaf motif on rolled seat front. Cane seat.

Dimensions: H. 34¼'' W. 17 7/8'' D. 19¾''
Materials: seat frame, maple; back posts and legs, birch
Date: c. 1836-1845
Marks: bronze stencil on back of seat frame, "W. COREY, PORTLAND, ME."
Courtesy of Earle G. Shettleworth, Jr., Gardiner, Me.
History: This chair was made in the factory of Walter Corey between 1842 and 1866 when he was established at 52 & 54 Exchange Street. Born in 1809 in Ashburton, Mass., Corey moved to Portland in 1836 and bought out cabinetmaker Nathaniel Ellsworth on Exchange Street. With Jonathan O. Bancroft, he opened a "cabinet warehouse". In 1842, Corey acquired the water rights at Great Falls on the Presumpscot River in Windham. There he built a factory for sawing, planing and turning. The pieces were then sent to Portland for assembly, finishing and shipment or sale. At its height the firm manufactured 20,000 chairs a year. Disaster struck in 1866. On June 16th, Corey's machine shop was gutted by fire, and less than a month later his whole Portland operation went up in flames when a huge fire swept the city. Temporary quarters were established on Kennebec Street at Back Cove. However, Corey was rapidly moving into distribution rather than manufacture and in 1870 completed the shift with the sale of his Windham operation. The business then became a showroom for household furnishings until it was finally dissolved in 1941.
Source: Barry and Shettleworth, "Walter Corey's Furniture Manufactory in Portland, Maine", *Antiques* (May, 1982), 1199-1205

Corey Windsor-Hitchcock Side Chair (right)

Black base coat with gold striping outlining major elements. Black-red comb grained seat. Gold banding on balls of legs, stretcher and back posts. Bronze stencil of rose and vines on rolled seat front. Silver, copper and gold stencil of Portland Harbor on crest rail.

Dimensions: H. 33'' W. 19¾'' D. 18 1/8''
Materials: seat, basswood; back posts and legs, beech; stretchers, birch
Date: 1842-1866
Marks: stencil on seat bottom, "WALTER COREY. 52 & 54 EXCHANGE ST. PORTLAND. ME."
Courtesy of Earle G. Shettleworth, Jr., Gardiner, Me.
History: See above.

Corey Klismos Type Vase-back Side Chair (left)

Rosewood graining with gold striping. Cane seat.

Dimensions: H. 34 7/8″ W. 18″ D. 19½″
Materials: seat frame, maple; legs and back upright, beech
Date: c. 1840-1850
Marks: bronze stencil on back of seat frame, "W. CORY. PORTLAND, ME."
Courtesy of Earle G. Shettleworth, Jr., Gardner, Me.
History: See Plate 26

Todd and Beckett Vase-back Side Chair (right)

Rosewood graining with bronze striping. Bronzed balls and rings on legs. Cane seat.

Dimensions: H. 34″ W. 17½″ D. 19¾″
Materials: seat frame and legs, birch
Date: c. 1844-1848
Marks: bronze stencil on back of seat frame, "TODD & BECKETT, 136 MIDDLE
　　　　ST., PORTLAND, ME."
MSM 75.61.3
History: James Todd was born in 1794 in Hingham, Mass. At the age of sixteen he
　　　　is said to have been apprenticed to Frenchman Paul Mondelli, a Boston
　　　　gilder and looking glass and picture frame manufacturer. Todd moved to
　　　　Portland in 1820 and set up his own looking glass and picture frame manu-
　　　　factory. In 1834, he took on Samuel S. Beckett as a partner; ten years later,
　　　　the two expanded into furniture manufacturing along with their past lines.
　　　　After 1848, Beckett disappeared from the Portland Directories, and Todd
　　　　continued on with sons James T. and William, both trained as gilders. In
　　　　1866, Todd's operation was destroyed in the Great Portland fire, the same
　　　　one that consumed the Corey operation.
Sources: FC, 1850: Me., r. 252, p. 123
　　　　MBD-1855
　　　　PD-1823, 1826, 1831, 1834, 1837, 1841, 1844, 1846, 1847-8, 1850-1, 1852-3,
　　　　　1856
　　　　Montgomery, *American Furniture: Federal Period,* pp. 482-483
　　　　Newspaper clipping in Scrap Book of Portland Obituaries (Vol. 9, p. 67)
　　　　　at Maine Historical Society

Slat-Back Chair

Ochre brown on cream graining in a wavy pattern. Seat missing.

Dimensions: H. 34½'' W. 18'' D. 15½''
Materials: seat frame, beech; legs, birch
Date: c. 1800-1820
MSM 70.112.7 Donated by Leroy F. Hussey, Augusta, Me.
History: The chair was acquired from a farm in the Vassalboro, Me. area.

Child's Armed Slat-Back Chair

Red and black graining. Rush seat.

Dimensions: H. 23'' W. 14'' D. 11¼''
Materials: seat frame, slats and stretchers, ash; legs and back posts, maple
Date: c. 1810-1830
MSM 80.20.14 Donated by George B. Jacobs, East Madison, Me.
History: The chair was acquired from the John K. Morrison homestead in East
         Madison, Me., which was built in the early nineteenth century.

Hudson and Brooks
Comb-Back Windsor Rocking Arm Chair

Painted yellow. Light red/brown banding and black/dark brown striping on crest rails. Wreathes, green leaves and gold scrolls on crest rails. Outline of design remains on splats, but color worn off. Arms unpainted.

Dimensions: H. 45″ W. 20¾″ D. 27″
Materials: pine and maple; arms, mahogany
Date: c. 1815-1823
Marks: printed paper label on seat bottom, "HUDSON & BROOKS, PORTLAND"
Collection of the Metropolitan Museum of Art, Gift of Mr. and Mrs. Arnold
  Skromme, 1971
History: The early careers of John Bradley Hudson (chairmaker and decorative
          painter) and John L. Brooks (chairmaker) are at this point unknown.
          The two first appear in an 1823 newspaper notice announcing the dissolu-
          tion of their partnership. After that date both continued on individually in
          their chosen trades until 1834, when John Hudson had gone to work for
          Jewett and Mudges, Portland brokers and furniture distributors and John
          Brooks had become a constable.
Sources: CCRD: 97,329; 106,304; 108,289
          ISMR: 4/5/1823
          PD-1823 (Thayer), 1823 (Jewett), 1827, 1831, 1834

White Salem Rocking Arm Chair

Red and black graining with yellow striping. Green banding on spindles and crest rail. Remains of green and yellow design on center of crest rail.

Dimensions: H. 41¾'' W. 18½'' D. 26½''
Materials: seat, basswood; back posts and crest rail, birch; arms and rockers, maple
Date: c. 1840-1849
Marks: printed paper label on chair bottom, ''WARRANTED CHAIRS BY SAMUEL K WHITE, EXETER, Me.''
MSM 79.8.1
History: See Plate 25

Tobey Boston Rocking Arm Chair

Red and black graining with yellow striping and bronze stenciling. Stencil on crest rail. Simulated bird's-eye maple seat. Arms unpainted. Roll on front of seat replaced. Striping on rockers similar to that on rockers of Tobey family rocking settee (Plate 32).

Dimensions: H. 43½'' W. 23'' D. 29¾''
Materials: seat, basswood; arm posts, birch; legs, back posts, crest rail and rockers, beech
Date: c. 1830-1845
MSM 81.96.4
History: See Plate 7.

Tobey Rocking Settee

Red and black graining with yellow striping and green banding. Rolled-front seat painted yellow. Bronze stenciled gate and crest rail. Striping on rockers similar to that on rockers of Tobey family rocking chair (Plate 31).

Dimensions: H. 33'' W. 56'' D. 27¼''
Materials: seat, basswood; back posts, birch; gate posts, maple; crest rail and gate, probably pine or basswood
Date: c. 1830-1845
MSM 81.102.1
History: See Plate 7

Bibliography

I. PRIMARY SOURCES

A. Manuscripts

Federal Census: 1850 (Maine). Microfilm. Maine State Archives, Augusta, Me.

Federal Census: 1850 (Maine). MSS. 47 vols. Maine State Archives, Augusta, Me.

Federal Industrial Census: 1850 (Maine). MSS. 1 vol. Maine State Archives, Augusta, Me.

Federal Industrial Census: 1870 (Maine). Microfilm. Maine State Archives, Augusta, Me.

Cumberland County Registry of Deeds. Portland, Me.

Kennebec County Registry of Deeds. Augusta, Me.

Kennebec County Registry of Probate. Augusta, Me.

Bath Makers Daybook, 1799 - 1805 [Bath, Me.]. MSS. Maine State Museum, Augusta, Me.

Brewer, John, Daybook, 1835 - 1837 [Brewer, Me.]. MSS. Old Sturbridge Village, Sturbridge, Mass.

Knowlton, David, Daybook, 1826 - 1835 [Augusta, Me.]. MSS. (Photocopy. Maine State Museum, Augusta, Me.)

Knowlton, Nathaniel, Daybook, 1812 - 1859 [Eliot, Me.]. MSS. Maine Historical Society, Portland, Me.

"Diary of Reverend Joseph Field: A Missionary Tour of the District of Maine [1805]." MSS. Kennebec Historical Society. (Photocopy at Maine State Museum, Augusta, Me.)

Brown, Christine. "Vital Records of Fairfield, Maine." Typescript. 1980. (at Maine State Library, Augusta, Me.)

Lilly, Georgiana H., and Hewin, Ella M. Old Book of Town Records, in "Chesterville, Maine, Records," ed. by Georgiana H. Lilly, 1941. (Typescript, Maine State Library, Augusta, Me.)

B. Printed

Conant, Ethel Colby, ed. *Vital Records of Augusta, Maine to the Year 1892.* Portland, Me.: Maine Historical Society, 1934.

Vital Records of Bridgewater, Massachusetts to the Year 1850. 2 vols. Boston: New England Historical and Genealogical Society, 1916.

Maine Register, 1873-74.

Maine Business Directories, 1855, 1869, 1874-75, 1880, 1885.

Bangor Directories, 1834, 1843, 1846, 1848, 1851.

Portland Directories, 1823 (Thayer), 1823 (Jewett), 1827, 1831, 1834, 1837, 1841, 1844, 1846, 1847-48, 1850-51, 1856, 1858-59, 1863-64.

Newspapers

Augusta Courier, 1831-32.

(Augusta) *Kennebec Journal,* 1825-1848.

(Augusta) *Maine Patriot and State Gazette,* 1823-1831.

Bangor Daily Whig and Courier, 1836-1850.

(Bangor) *Penobscot Journal,* 1831-32.

Bangor Register, 1815-1820, 1822-1831.

Bangor Register and Penobscot Advertiser, 1821-22.

(Bath) *Maine Enquirer and Lincoln County Advertiser,* 1832-33.

(Bath) *Maine Gazette,* 1822.

(Bath) *Maine Inquirer,* 1827.

Belfast Gazette, 1826-27.

(Belfast) *Hancock Gazette and Penobscot Patriot,* 1820-1826.

(Belfast) *Republican Journal,* 1829-1850.

Ellsworth American, 1855-1860.

(Ellsworth) *The Radical,* 1835-36.

(Gardiner) *Christian Intelligencer and Eastern Chronicle,* 1826-1834.

(Hallowell) *American Advocate,* 1810-1823, 1833-1834.

Hallowell Gazette, 1814-1824.

Lewiston Falls Journal, 1843-1850.

(Paris) *Oxford Democrat,* 1846-1857.

(Portland) *Eastern Argus,* 1803-1815, 1824-1835.

(Portland) *Independent Statesman and Maine Republican,* 1823.

(Portland) *Jefferson,* 1834-35.

(Portland) *Oriental Trumpet,* 1797.

Portland Advertiser, 1827, 1859.

Portland Gazette, 1798-1824.

Portland Transcript, 1837-1850.

(Rockland) *United States Democrat,* 1857.

(Saco) *Maine Palladium,* 1826-1829.

(Thomaston) *Limerock Gazette,* 1846.

(Winthrop) *Maine Farmer,* 1833-1850.

Hepplewhite, George. *The Cabinet-Maker and Upholsterer's Guide.* 3rd. ed. London: I. & J. Taylor, 1974 (reprinted by Dover Publications, New York, 1969).

Sheraton, Thomas. *The Cabinet Dictionary.* 2 vols. London: W. Smith, 1803 (reprinted by Praeger Publishers, New York, 1970).

Sheraton, Thomas. *The Cabinet-Maker and Upholsterer's Drawing Book.* 3rd. ed. London: T. Bensley, 1802 (reprinted by Praeger Publishers, New York, 1970).

The Artist's Companion and Manufacturer's Guide. Boston: J. Norman, 1814.

The Mechanic's Assistant, Being a Select Collection of Valuable Receipts. Utica, New York: D. Bennett and Co., 1830.

Porter, Rufus, *Select Collection of Approved, Genuine and Modern Receipts.* Concord, Massachusetts: J.T. Peters, (ca. 1824).

Tingry, P.F., *Painter's and Colourman's Complete Guide.* 3rd ed. London: Sherwood, Gilbert and Peper, 1830.

Tingry, P.F., *The Varnisher's Guide.* London: Sherwood, Gilbert and Peper, 1832.

Whittock, Nathaniel, *The Decorative Painters' and Glaziers' Guide.* London: Isaac Taylor Hinton, 1828.

Howard, Daniel, and Town, Thomas. [Broadside for Clocks], Belfast, Me., 1847. (Photocopy at Maine State Museum).

"Corey's Furniture Manufactory," *Portland Transcript,* April 27, 1850.

"Labor Saving Machinery and Increase of Manufacturing at A. & E. Dole Furniture Manufactory," *Bangor Daily Whig and Courier,* July 7, 1843.

"Memoir and Journals of Rev. Paul Coffin, D.D., of Buxton, Me." Maine Historical Society, *Collections,* 1st ser. IV (1856), 239-405.

II. Secondary Sources

Banks, Ronald F. *Maine Becomes A State: The Movement to Separate Maine From Massachusetts, 1785 - 1820.* Middletown, Connecticut: Wesleyan University Press, 1970.

Barry, William D., and Shettleworth, Earle G., Jr. "Walter Corey's Furniture Manufactory in Portland, Maine." *Antiques* (May 1982), 1199-1205.

Butler, Francis G. *A History of Farmington, Franklin County, Maine.* Farmington: Press of Knowlton, McLeary, and Co., 1885.

Churchill, Edwin A., et al. *Landmark of Service: Chapters in the History of Methodism in Augusta, 1828 - 1978.* Augusta, Maine: The Green Street Methodist Church, 1978.

Cooper, Wendy A. *In Praise of America: American Decorated Arts, 1650 - 1830.* New York: Knopf, 1980.

Fales, Dean A., Jr. *American Painted Furniture, 1660 - 1880.* New York: E.P. Dutton and Company, Inc., 1972.

Frazer, Esther Stevens. "Painted Furniture in America: The Sheraton Fancy Chair, 1790 - 1817." *Antiques* (June 1924), 302-306.

Frazer, Esther Stevens. "Painted Furniture in America: II: The Period of Stencilling, 1817 - 1835." *Antiques* (September 1924), 141-146.

Frazer, Esther Stevens. "The Golden Age of Stencilling." *Antiques* (April 1922), 162-163.

Giffen, Jane C. "Susanna Rowson and Her Academy." *Antiques* (September 1970), 436-440.

Groce, George C., and Wallace, David H. *The New York Historical Society's Dictionary of Artists in America, 1564 - 1860.* New Haven and London: Yale University Press, 1957.

Hayden, Charles Albert, comp. *The Capen Family: Descendants of Bernard Capen of Dorchester, Mass.,* revised by Jessie Hale Tuttle. Minneapolis: Augsburg Publishing House, 1829.

Hunter, Dard. *Paper Making.* New York: Dover Publications, Inc., 1943.

Jackson, Ronald Vern, and Teeples, Gary Ronald, eds. *Maine 1840 Census Index.* Bountiful, Utah: Accelerated Indexing Systems, Inc., 1978.

Jackson, Ronald Vern, Teeples, Gary Ronald, and Schaefermeyer, David, eds. *Maine, 1810 Census Index.* Bountiful, Utah: Accelerated Indexing System, Inc., 1976.

Jackson, Ronald Vern, Teeples, Gary Ronald, and Schaefermeyer, David, eds. *Maine 1820 Census Index.* Bountiful, Utah: Accelerated Indexing Systems, Inc., 1976.

John, W.D., and Simcox, Anne. *Pontypool and Usk-Japanned Wares.* Bath, England: Harding and Curtis Ltd., 1953.

Kenney, John T. *The Hitchcock Chair.* New York: Clarkson N. Potter, Inc., 1971.

Koizumi, G. *Lacquer Work.* London: Sir Isaac Pitman and Sons, Ltd., 1923.

Lamson, William J. *Descendants of William Lamson of Ipswich, Mass., 1634-1917.* New York: Tobias A. Wright, 1917.

Landscape in Maine, 1820-1970: A Sesquicentennial Exhibition. n.p., 1970.

Lea, Zilla Rides, ed. *The Ornamental Chair: Its Development in America (1700-1890).* Rutland, Vermont: Charles E. Tuttle Company, 1960.

Lipman, Jean. *Rufus Porter: Yankee Pioneer.* New York: Clarkson N. Potter, Inc., 1968.

Maine Charitable Mechanics Association. *Constitution and History of the Maine Charitable Mechanics Association.* Portland: Published by the Association, 1965.

Maine Forestry Department. *Forest Trees of Maine.* Bulletin 24. Augusta, Maine: Maine Forestry Department, 1973.

Marini, Stephen. *Radical Sects of Revolutionary New England.* Cambridge: Harvard University Press, 1982.

Marini, Stephen. "Religion in Maine, 1783-1820." Paper presented at "Maine and Statehood: A Symposium for Scholars," sponsored by the Maine Humanities Council, Portland, Maine, December 3, 1982.

McCann, Michael. *Artist Beware.* New York: Watson-Guptil Publications, 1979.

McKearin, Helen, "The Case of the Pressed Glass Knobs," *Antiques* (August 1951), 118-120.

Mitchell and Davis, comp. *The Fairfield Register, 1904.* Kents Hill, Maine: H.E. Mitchell, Co., 1904.

Mitchell and Davis, comp. *The Paris Register, 1906.* Brunswick, Maine: H.E. Mitchell, Co., 1906.

Montgomery, Charles F. *American Furniture: The Federal Period.* New York: Viking Press, 1966.

Morrill's Auctions, Inc. *Early American Country Antiques at Public Auction. Christopher Huntington Collection.* Portland: Portland Lithograph Co., 1974.

Murry, Maria D. *The Art of Tray Painting.* New York: Bramhall House, 1954.

North, James W. *The History of Augusta.* Augusta, Maine: Clapp and North, 1870.

Obituary (of James Todd). Newspaper clipping in Scrapbook of Portland Obituaries, vol. 9, p. 67. Maine Historical Society.

Obituary (of Jepheth Beale). *KJ,* February 27, 1867.

Panshin, A.J., and de Zeeuw, Carl. *Textbook of Wood Technology.* 3rd ed. New York: McGraw-Hill, 1970.

Parker, N. Grier. "John White, Chairmaker and Decorator." *The Decorator,* vol. VI, no. 1 (1952), 15-16.

Pennington, Samuel, "Guptill Family Estate Auction." *Maine Antiques Digest* (October 1982), 1B-2B.

Plain and Elegant, Rich and Common: Documented New Hampshire Furniture, 1750-1850. Concord: New Hampshire Historical Society, 1979.

Rumford, Beatrix T., ed. *American Folk Portraits.* Boston: New York Graphic Society in association with the Colonial Williamsburg Foundation, 1981.

Santore, Charles. *The Windsor Style in America.* Philadelphia, Pennsylvania: Running Press, 1981.

Sewall, Oliver. History of Chesterville, Maine, in "Chesterville-Maine, Records," ed. by Georgiana H. Lilly, 1941 (typescript, Maine State Library).

Shettleworth, Earle G., Jr. "The Radford Brothers: Portland Cabinetmakers of the Federal Period." *Antiques* (August 1974), 285-287.

Spalding, Charles W. *The Spalding Memorial: A Genealogical History of Edward Spalding of Virginia and Massachusetts Bay, and His Descendants.* Chicago: American Publication Association, 1897.

Stocking, Charles Henry Wright. *The History and Genealogy of the Knowltons of England and America.* New York: Knickerbocker Press, 1897.

Thomas, Gertrude Z. "Lacquer: Chinese, Indian, 'Right' Japan and American." *Antiques* (June 1961), 572-575.

Waring, Janet. *Early American Stencils on Walls and Furniture.* New York: Dover Publications, Inc., 1968. (Reprint of 1837 publication by William R. Scott.)

White, Almira L. *Genealogy of Descendants of John White of Wenham and Lancaster, Mass., 1638-1900.* 3 vols. Haverhill, Massachusetts: Charles Brothers, Printer, 1900.

Williamson, Joseph. *History of the City of Belfast.* 2 vols. Portland: Loring, Short, and Harmon, 1877.

Decorator Checklist

Known or Probable Furniture Decorators*

ALDES, W.
w. Belfast, 1841; house, sign, and sleigh painter.
RJ: 9/17/1841.

BANGS, JAMES F.
b. Mass.; w. Portland, 1850; age 32 in 1850; chair painter.
FC, 1850: Me., r. 252, p. 103

BEALE, CHANDLER
b. 1817; w. Augusta, 1846-1857+; d. 1904; son of JEPHETH BEALE; 1846-1852 with JOSHUA HEATH; 1857 with JOSEPH FARNHAM, Augusta painter. (See HEATH & BEALE; FARNHAM, JOSEPH)
FC, 1850: Me., r. 256, p. 20
KCRD: 145,108; 151,64; 153,326; 159,212; 182,504; 210,333
KCRP: 31,9280
KJ: 2/20/1846; 3/24/1848

BEALE, HORATIO
w. Augusta, 1824-1825; w. Bangor, 1825-1834; friends with MOSES WELLS, cabinetmaker, in Augusta, 1825; painter and cabinet and chairmaker. (See MOORE & BEALE)
KCRD: 50,176; 52,215; 56,61; 61,120; 63,98; 67,378
BR: 6/30/1829
BD: 1834

BEALE, JEPHETH
b. Bridgewater, Mass., 1781; w. Augusta, 1814-1819, 1835-1863; d. 1863; brother of OLIVER SALEM BEALE; father of CHANDLER BEALE; arrived in Augusta in 1801; chairmaker and painter; listed as yeoman in 1819-1835; partner of Elihu Robinson, Augusta chairmaker, 1836-1839 (?); early leader of Augusta Methodist Society.
FC, 1850: Me., r. 256, p. 20
KCRD: 7,429; 16,346; 23,178; 106,231; 107,334; 111,317; 152,37; 200,67
Vital Records of Bridgewater, Mass., I, 47
KJ: 2/27/1863
Churchill, et al., *Landmark of Service,* pp. 4-5, 15
North, *Augusta,* pp. 286-89.

BEALE, OLIVER SALEM
b. Bridgewater, Mass., 1776; w. Augusta, 1829-1832; w. Bangor, 1832(?)-1851; brother of JEPHETH BEALE; sign, chaise, and fancy painter and gilder; imitated wood, marble, mahogany, oak, birch, maple; 1829 ordained as first minister of the Green Street United Methodist Church; moved to Bangor, 1832; building carriages with partner William P. Osgood, 1843-1845; painting in 1845; Daguerreotypist in 1846; carriage and sign painter, 1848-1850(+).

Jackson, et al., *Maine, 1810 Census Index*
KCRD: 78,169; 96,483; 214,338
Vital Records of Bridgewater, Mass., I, 47
AC: 8/19/1831; 12/22/1831; 8/10/1832
KJ: 9/24/1830; 12/17/1830; 5/20/1831
MPSG: 10/27/1830: 11/17/1830
BD: 1843, 1846, 1848, 1851
David Knowlton's Daybook, April 10 and 27, 1830; October 14, 1831, etc.
Churchill, et al., *Landmark of Service,* pp. 4, 5, 15
North, *Augusta,* pp. 286-89

BELL & TOWNLEY
w. Portland, 1846; house, ship, and ornamental painters; painted wood and marble imitations; predecessors of TOWNLEY, DAVIS & CO. (See TOWNLEY, DAVIS & CO.)
PT: 6/20/1846

BENNETT, WILLIAM
w. Ellsworth, 1835. (See WILLIAM BENNETT & CO.; TREWORTHY & CHAMBERLAIN)
TR: 6/2/1835, 8/21/1835

BENNETT, WILLIAM, & CO.
w. Ellsworth, 1835; cabinet and chairmakers; carriage repairers and painters; WILLIAM BENNETT & CO. dissolved 6/28/1835; predecessor to TREWORTHY & CHAMBERLAIN. (See TREWORTHY & CHAMBERLAIN)
TR: 6/2/1835, 8/21/1835

BLANCHARD, SAMUEL
w. Bangor, 1836; continued as painter, glazier, and chairmaker after partnership of NEWHALL & BLANCHARD dissolved 6/9/1836. (See NEWHALL & BLANCHARD)
BDWC: 6/15/1836, 7/2/1836

BROOKS, GARDINER
w. Bangor, 1828-1829; chairmaker and painter; "Keeps on hand: fancy and common chairs, rocking chairs, children's chairs. Old chairs mended and repainted at short notice."
BR: 11/18/1828, 11/17/1829

BURPEE, N. A.
w. E. Thomaston, 1846. (See BURPEE, N. A. & S. H.)
LRG: 1/7/1846

BURPEE, N. A. & S. H.
w. E. Thomaston, 1846; house, ship, sign, and ornamental painters and glaziers; furniture makers.
LRG: 1/7/1846

---

* It should be noted that the names of a number of known makers of Maine decorated furniture (e.g., William Mason of Fryeburg; Jonathan Raynes of Lewiston Falls; Madison Tuck of Hallowell, Maine) are not present on this list. They have not been included because evidence has not yet been located which indicates that they decorated the furniture which they made.

BURPEE, SAMUEL H.
w. E. Thomaston, 1846; w. Rockland, 1850; age 32 in 1850. (See BURPEE, N. A. & S. H.)

    FC, 1850: Me., r. 259, p. 93
    LRG: 1/7/1846

BUTLER, GEORGE W.
w. Portland, 1850s; age 28 in 1850; chair painter.

    FC, 1850: Me., r. 252, p. 104

CAPEN, WILLIAM J.
b. 1802; w. Portland, 1823-1859; d. 1863; sign, ornamental and chair painter; chairmaking from 1823-1826; gave up chairmaking in 1827 and only painted; partnership with John Carr in 1835; customs inspector from 1850-1853; returned to painting in 1856; died of "painter's colic." (See CARR & CAPEN)

    FC, 1850: Me., r. 252, p. 92
    FC, 1860: Me., r, 436, p. 217
    EA: 10/31/1824; 11/1/1824; 1/6/1825; 3/15/1833;
      6/3/1833
    J: 9/7/1835
    PA: 7/29/1827; 10/4/1859
    PT: 4/28/1849; 3/28/1863
    PD: 1823; 1826; 1831; 1834; 1837; 1841; 1844;
      1846; 1847-48; 1850-51; 1852-53; 1856; 1858-
      1859; 1863-1864
    Hayden, *Capen Family,* pp. 138, 208
    Constitution and History of the Maine Charitable
    Mechanics Association, p. 81

CARR, (JOHN) & CAPEN (WILLIAM Jr.)
w. Portland, 1835; sign and fancy painters.

    J: 9/7/1835

CARR, JOHN
w. Portland, 1835 (See CARR & CAPEN)

    J: 9/7/1835

CHAMBERLAIN, CHARLES E. P.
w. Ellsworth, 1835; age 38 in 1850; joiner. (See WILLIAM BENNETT & CO; TREWORTHY & CHAMBERLAIN)

    FC, 1850: Me., r. 255, p. 304
    Ells. Am.: 7/17/1835; 8/21/1835
    TR: 8/21/1835

CLEAVES, ISRAEL
w. Saco, 1826; repaired and painted carriages; wagon, sleigh, cabinet and chairmaker.

    MP: 8/16/1826

CODMAN, CHARLES
b. Portland, 1800; w. 1822-1842; d. 1842; moved from Boston in 1822 as a "military, standard, fancy, ornamental and sign painter"; produced commercial work during these years in order to survive financially.

    EA: 7/28/1829
    Landscape in Maine, 1820-1970: A Sesquicentennial
      Exhibition, n.p., 1970, p. 10.

DAVIS, H.
w. Portland, 1849. (See TOWNLEY, DAVIS & CO.)

    PT: 10/27/1849

DOE, HOWARD D.
w. Augusta, 1848; age 35 in 1850; painter, glazier, and grainer; shop in building known as the "Old Castle."

    FC, 1850: Me., r. 256, p. 102
    KJ: 4/28/1848

ELLIOT, ANDREW
w. Portland, 1850; painter and cabinetmaker.

    FC, 1850: Me., r. 252, p. 237

FAIRBANKS, W.
w. Bangor, 1842; chair manufacturer; "(Hand) ornamental painting done to order at short notice."

    BDWC: 6/1/1842

FARNHAM, JOSEPH
w. Augusta, 1847-1857; painter. (See BEALE, CHANDLER).

    KCRD: 153,335; 158,351; 191,476; 210,333; 211,381

FLAGNER, THOMAS
w. Belfast, 1823. (See PHILLIPS & FLAGNER)

    HGPP: 7/2/1823

FLEMENT, LEWIS
w. Bangor, 1850; painter and varnisher at SHAW & MERRILL.

    BD: 1843, 1851

FRAZIER, ISAAC
w. Ellsworth, 1856; house, ship, sign, and ornamental painter; he stated that "Particular attention paid to Graining, Varnishing, Polishing, Ornamenting and Enameling."

    Ells. Am.: 6/20/1856

FROST, NATHANIEL
w. Portland, 1803; "Made Fancy, Bamboo and Windsor chairs and settees"; old chairs repaired and painted.

    EA: 9/8/1803

GILMAN, JOHN K.
w. Hallowell, 1822; coach, chaise, sign and house painter; gilder, glazier, and varnisher; Japan and copal varnish used.

    HG: 1/30/1822; 5/29/1822

HAGGET, JOHN
w. Portland, 1818-1819; chairmaker, repairer, and painter. (See VERY & HAGGET)

 PG: 11/16/1819

HAMBLIN, ALMERY
w. Portland, 1820s-1841+; house, sign, and ornamental painter in business with his four sons, JOSEPH G., NATHANIEL, ELI, and STURTEVANT J.; daughter, Rosamond, married WILLIAM MATTHEW PRIOR in 1828. (See PRIOR, WILLIAM MATTHEW)

 Rumford, Beatrix T., ed., *American Folk Portraits,* Boston: New York Graphic Society in association with the Colonial Williamsburg Foundation, 1981, p. 112

HAMBLIN, ELI
b. c. 1804; w. Portland, 1820s-1839; d. 1839; brother of JOSEPH G., NATHANIEL, and STURTEVANT J.; brother-in-law of WILLIAM MATTHEW PRIOR; in business with his father, ALMERY, and brothers as house, sign and ornamental painters. (See PRIOR, WILLIAM MATTHEW)

 Rumford, *American Folk Paintings,* p. 112
 Groce, George C. and Wallace, David H., *The New York Historical Society's Dictionary of Artists in America, 1564-1860;* New Haven and London: Yale University Press, 1957, p. 286

HAMBLIN, GEORGE
w. Gorham, 1763+; painter and glazier; father of ALMERY; grandfather of ELI, JOSEPH G., NATHANIEL and STURTEVANT J.; moved to Maine from Barnstable, Mass. in 1763.

 Rumford, *American Folk Portraits,* p. 112

HAMBLIN, JOSEPH G.
b. c. 1817; w. Portland, 1820s-1841+; brother of ELI, NATHANIEL and STURTEVANT J.; brother-in-law of WILLIAM MATTHEW PRIOR; moved to Boston, Mass., in 1841 with his brothers, WILLIAM PRIOR and his family. (See HAMBLIN, ALMERY; HAMBLIN, ELI; PRIOR, WILLIAM MATTHEW)

 Rumford, *American Folk Portraits,* p. 112
 Groce and Wallace, *Dictionary of Artists in America,* p. 286.

HAMBLIN, NATHANIEL
w. Portland, 1820s-1841+; brother of ELI, JOSEPH G. and STURTEVANT; brother-in-law of WILLIAM MATTHEW PRIOR; moved to Boston, Mass. in 1841 with his brothers, WILLIAM PRIOR and his family. (See HAMBLIN, ALMERY; HAMBLIN, ELI; PRIOR, WILLIAM MATTHEW)

 Rumford, *American Folk Portraits,* p. 112
 Groce and Wallace, *Dictionary of Artists in America,* p. 286

HAMBLIN, STURTEVANT J.
w. Portland, 1820s-1841+; brother of ELI, JOSEPH G. and NATHANIEL; brother-in-law of WILLIAM MATTHEW PRIOR; moved to Boston, Mass. in 1841 with his brothers, WILLIAM PRIOR and his family where he began a career as a portrait painter. (See HAMBLIN, ALVERY; HAMBLIN, ELI; PRIOR, WILLIAM MATTHEW)

 Rumford, *American Folk Portraits,* p. 112
 Groce and Wallace, *Dictionary of Artists in America,* pp. 286-87.

HARDY, JOHN
w. Bangor, 1850; age 33 in 1850; chair gilder.

 FC, 1850: Me., r. 264, p. 74

HASKELL, WILLIAM S.
w. Augusta, 1842-43; age 40 in 1850; gilder, in business with MOSES WELLS, cabinetmaker. (See WELLS & HASKELL)

 FC, 1850: Me., r. 256, p. 16
 KJ: 12/2/1842

HEATH, JOSHUA L.
b. 1810; w. Augusta, 1833-1852(+?); age 40 in 1850; house, ship, and sign painter. (See HEATH & BEALE)

 FC, 1850: Me., r. 256, p. 2
 KCRD: 78,299; 113,494; 161,85; 161,361; 179,376
 KJ: 2/20/1846; 3/24/1848

HEATH, (JOSHUA L.) & BEALE (CHANDLER)
w. Augusta, 1846-1852(+); house, ship and sign painters; graining, papering and glazing; advertised on 3/9/1848 that they had employed a graining specialist who had "practice in Boston and Lowell."

 KCRD: 159,212; 182,504
 KJ: 2/20/1846; 3/24/1848

HINCH, JAMES
w. Thomaston, 1857; "White enameling, graining, polishing and all kinds of gilding, ornamenting and fancy painting for ships' cabins. Also house and sign painting, marbling."

 USD: 11/5/1857

HOLLAND, FRANCIS
w. Portland, 1848-1851; trained GEORGE LORD who came to COREY BROTHERS, Portland, in 1848; HOLLAND gave LORD his "best stencils"; returned to Boston in 1851.

 Waring, *Early American Stencils,* p. 121

HOLT [NELSON] & CO.
w. Bangor, 1851; painters and manufacturers of furniture.

 BD: 1851, 19

HOLT, NELSON
w. Bangor, 1851; painter. (See HOLT & CO.)

 BD: 1851

HUDSON [JOHN BRADLEY] & BROOKS [JOHN L.]
w. Portland, 1820-1823; JOHN BRADLEY HUDSON listed as chair painter in 1823 city directory; in partnership with JOHN L. BROOKS, chair maker; dissolved, April 1823.

> ISMR: 4/5/1823
> PD: 1823

HUDSON, JOHN BRADLEY
w. Portland, 1823-1834; fancy and sign painter in shop of GEORGE CLARK, cabinetmaker, in 1827. (See HUDSON & BROOKS)

> CCRD: 97,329; 106,304; 108,289
> EA: 1/23/1827
> ISMR: 4/5/1823
> PD: 1823, 1827, 1831, 1834

KNOWLTON, NATHANIEL
b. Eliot, 1791; w. Eliot, 1815-1859; age 60 in 1850; d. 1863; apprenticed with Benjamin Lamson, Boston cabinetmaker, in 1814; started in 1815 as his own cabinet and carriage maker and painter; later shifted to vehicle manufacturing and painting.

> FC, 1850: Me., r. 274, p. 255
> Nathaniel Knowlton's Day Book, 1812-1859, 2 vols.
> Lamson, Descendants of William Lamson, p. 127
> Stocking, Knowltons, p. 148

LORD, GEORGE
b. 1833; w. Portland, 1848-1925; d. 1928; fancy painting, graining, striping, and stenciling of furniture; trained by FRANCIS HOLLAND; came to COREY BROTHERS in 1848; HOLLAND gave LORD his "best stencils."

> Waring, Early American Stencils, p. 121

MARSTON, GIDEON
w. Bangor, 1841-1842; age 39 in 1850 (See NASH & MARSTON)

> FC, 1850: Me., r. 264, p. 91
> BDWC: 12/14/1841; 5/18/1842

McDOUGALL, HUGH
w. Hallowell, 1810; sign and ornamental painter and gilder; repainted and varnished old chaises; worked in connection with William Jordan, chaise maker.

> AA: 5/8/1810

MESERVEY, JOHN
w. Bangor, 1832-1884; sign and fancy painter; furniture (chairs) manufacturer.

> PJ: 2/28/1832
> BD: 1843, 1851, 1859-1860, 1871-1872, 1873-1874, 1875-1876, 1877-1878, 1880, 1884

MOORE, AMAZIAH S.
w. Augusta, 1824-1825; w. Bangor, 1825-1829 (+?); painter and glazier. (See MOORE & BEALE)

> KCRD: 50,176; 59,260; 63,292; 70,152
> BR: 1/20/1829

MOORE [AMAZIAH S.] & BEALE [HORATIO]
w. Bangor, 1825-1828; painters and glaziers; chair-makers; used copal and Japan varnishes; 4/20/26 occupied a part of shop owned and occupied by Edmund Dole, cabinetmaker; partnership dissolved 12/1/1828.

> BR: 5/5/1825; 4/20/1826; 6/29/1826; 12/28/1826; 12/10/1827; 4/22/1828; 11/4/1828

NASH, SIMON H.
w. Bangor, 1841-1842. (See NASH & MARSTON)

> BDWC: 12/14/1841, 5/18/1842

NASH, [SIMON H.] & MARSTON [GIDEON]
w. Bangor, 1841-1842; house, ship, sign and fancy painters; chair manufacturers, painters, and glaziers; new establishment, 5/17/1841, formerly occupied by Longfellow & Nash.

> BDWC: 12/14/1841; 5/18/1842

NEWHALL [SAMUEL C.] & BLANCHARD [SAMUEL]
w. Bangor, 1830s; painters, glaziers, and chair manufacturers; partnership dissolved 6/9/1836; business carried on by BLANCHARD. (See BLANCHARD, SAMUEL)

> BDWC: 6/15/1836; 7/2/1836

NEWHALL, SAMUEL C.
w. Bangor, 1830s. (See NEWHALL & BLANCHARD)

> BDWC: 6/16/1836

PARK, E. L.
w. Bangor, 1825. (See PARK, I. R. & E. L.)

> BR: 3/17/1825; 7/7/1825

PARK, I. R. [ISAAC] & E. L.
w. Bangor, 1825; house, sign and ornamental painters and glaziers; partners from 3/17/1825 - 7/4/1825.

> BR: 3/17/1825; 7/7/1825

PARK, ISAAC
w. Bangor, 1825-1829; house, sign and ornamental painter and glazier; partner of E. L. PARK from 3/17/1825-7/4/1825; left his shop by mid-1827, and was roofing by 3/25/1838; returned to painting and glazing 11/17/1829; moved to Dixfield and listed as a carpenter in 1850 census. (See PARK, I.R. & E.L.; WATERMAN, HENRY P & CO.; WOOD, ORLANDO T.)

> FC, 1850: Me., r. 263, p. 217
> BR: 3/17/1825; 7/7/1825; 12/29/1825; 4/13/1826; 6/29/1826; 12/21/1826; 4/11/1827; 8/8/1827; 1/16/1828; 3/25/1828; 4/22/1828; 11/17/1829

PARKER, ORIN
w. Augusta, 1850; chair trimmer.

> FC, 1850: Me., r. 256, p. 11

PERRY, LEONARD
w. Portland, 1806; coach, chaise, and sign painter
and gilder in the loft of Babcock & Child, who were
coach and chaise makers; used copal varnish and
Japan.

EA: 3/21/1806

PHILLIPS, NICHOLAS
w. Belfast, 1823. (See PHILLIPS & FLAGNER)

HGPP: 7/2/1823

PHILLIPS [Nicholas] & FLAGNER [Thomas]
w. Belfast, 1823; house, ship, and sign painters; also
painted masonic flooring and aprons, tablets for looking glasses, and other painting on glass, and chair
painting.

HGPP: 7/2/1823

PHILLIPS, WARREN
w. Portland, 1850; age 37 in 1850; chair painter.

FC, 1850: Me., r. 252, p. 103

PORTER, RUFUS
b. W. Boxford, Mass., 1792; w. Portland, 1810-1812;
w. Denmark, 1813; d. 1884; house and sign painter;
painted sleighs and drums in Denmark; possibly he
painted some furniture during these years; Fig. 47 in
Rufus Porter, Yankee Pioneer, shows a chest with
decorative painting, of the Porter school.

Lipman, *Rufus Porter: Yankee Pioneer,* pp. 89-158

PRIOR, WILLIAM MATTHEW
w. Bath, 1827; fancy, sign, and ornamental painter;
Prior is famous as a folk painter; worked with
HAMBLIN family.

MI: 10/16/1827

RACKLIFF, JOSEPH J.
w. Bath, 1833; coach, chaise, house, ship and sign
painter.

MELCA: 4/5/1833

ROBINSON, A.
w. Belfast, 1823-1825; moved to Hallowell, 1825;
house, ship, chaise and sign painter; "Masonic Flooring, Aprons, &c.; Japanning, Lackering, Gilting,
Bronzing and Varnishing"; other types of plain and
ornamental painting; worked in Hallowell loft over
Samuel W. Drew's chaise maker shop; originally of
A. & Z. Robinson; may be ALVAN ROBINSON, Portland, Nov. 19, 1822.

AA: 7/15/1825
HGPP: 7/9/1823

ROBINSON, ALVAN
w. Portland, 1822; sign painter and ornamental work
of all kinds; possibly A. ROBINSON, Belfast, 1823-
1825.

PG: 11/19/1822

SAFFORD, HIRAM
w. Augusta, 1831-1832. (See SAFFORD, M & H)

SAFFORD, M[icah] & H[iram]
w. Augusta, 1831-1832; chairmakers, painters and
glaziers; took over shop of MOSES SAFFORD, Jr.,
cabinetmaker; partnership dissolved 7/3/1832.

AC: 7/5/1832
KJ: 1/6/1832
MPSG: 4/27/1831

SAFFORD, MICAH
w. Augusta, 1832; continued as chairmaker, painter,
and glazier after partnership with HIRAM SAFFORD
ended 7/3/1832. (See SAFFORD, M & H)

AC: 7/5/1832

SAFFORD, MOSES, Jr.
w. Augusta, 1825-1831; age 56 in 1850; cabinet and
chairmaker; sold copal and Japan varnishes; MICAH
& HIRAM SAFFORD took over his shop in 1831.

FC, 1850: Me., r. 256, p. 30
KJ: 1/8/1825; 4/28/1827; 10/16/1829; 11/10/1829;
3/11/1831

SARGENT, LEWIS
w. Hallowell, 1814; chaise, sign and ornamental
painter; worked in shop of Levi Chadbourn, carriage
and chairmaker.

AA: 4/9/1814
HG: 4/13/1814

SIMONDS, JOSEPH
w. Waterville, 1844-1845; age 37 in 1850; furniture
manufacturer; painter and repairer of old furniture
at the sign of the BIG CHAIR.

FC, 1850: Me., r. 258, p. 102
KJ: 12/27/1844

SMILEY, DEAN
w. Hallowell, 1822-1823; house and ship painter;
chair manufacturer.

HG: 12/25/1822; 3/12/1823

SMITH, J. B.
w. Bath, 1833; house, ship and sign painter; glazier.

MELCA: 4/5/1833

SMITH, SAMUEL
w. Augusta, 1829-1832; cabinet furniture manufacturer; mahogany and painted parlor, kitchen, and
chamber furniture.

KJ: 1/16/1829; 3/6/1829; 7/31/1829; 11/6/1829;
3/5/1830; 5/5/1830; 1/28/1831; 9/30/1831; 2/10/1832;
7/20/1832

STEWART, DANIEL
b. Mass., 1786; w. Backus Corner, Farmington,
1812-1827; d. 1827; cabinet and chairmaker and
painter.

KCRP: S15
Maker's label (MSM file)

Francis G. Butler, *A History of Farmington, Franklin County, Maine*, Farmington: Press of Knowlton, McLeary, & Co., 1885, pp. 576-578
Charles Santore, *The Windsor Style in America*, Philadelphia, Pa.: Running Press, 1981, p. 51

TILTON, J. R.
w. Portland, 1849; banner, sign, and ornamental painter.

PT: 6/16/1849

TODD, JAMES
w. Portland, 1823-1856; age 55 in 1850; chamber furniture painter and maker; chairs repaired and painted; burnish gilder; looking glass maker; father of JAMES T. and WILLIAM TODD; worked with son, James T. (Todd & Son) from 1850-1856. (See TODD & BECKETT)

FC, 1850: Me., r. 252, p. 123
PT: 2/24/1849
Maine Business Directory, 1855.
PD: 1823; 1826; 1831; 1834; 1837; 1841; 1844; 1846; 1847-1848; 1850-1851; 1852-1853; 1856
Montgomery, F., *American Furniture: Federal Period*, pp. 273-274
Newspaper clipping in scrapbook of Portland obituaries (Vol. 9, p. 67) at Maine Historical Society.

TODD [JAMES] & BECKETT [SAMUEL S.]
w. Portland, 1834-1848; furniture (especially chairs) makers, painters, and burnish gilders.

PT: 2/24/1849
PD: 1834; 1837; 1841; 1844; 1846; 1847-1848

TODD, JAMES T.
w. Portland, 1847-1856; age 25 in 1850; gilder; son of JAMES TODD; brother of WILLIAM TODD; working with father (Todd & Son) from 1850-1856.

FC, 1850: Me., r. 252, p. 123
PD: 1847-1848, 1850-1851; 1852-1853; 1856

TODD, WILLIAM
w. Portland, 1852-1856; age 20 in 1850; burnish gilder; son of JAMES TODD; brother of JAMES T. TODD.

FC, 1850: Me., r. 252, p. 123
PD: 1852-1853, 1856

TOWNLEY, DAVIS & CO.
w. Portland, 1849; house, ship, sign and fancy painters; every branch of painting and graining; imitations of woods, marbles, graining; successors of BELL & TOWNLEY. (See BELL & TOWNLEY)

PT: 10/27/1849

TOWNLEY, SAMUEL
b. England; w. Portland, 1849; age 38 in 1850. (See BELL & TOWNLEY; TOWNLEY, DAVIS & CO.)

FC, 1850: Me., r. 252, p. 59
PT: 10/27/1849

TRASK, JOHN
w. Portland, 1850; age 44 in 1850; painter and cabinetmaker.

FC, 1850: Me., r. 252, p. 239

TREWORTHY [John] & CHAMBERLAIN [Charles E. P.]
w. Ellsworth, 1835; cabinet and chairmakers; carriage painters and repairers; successors of WILLIAM BENNETT & CO., which dissolved 8/21/1835. (See BENNETT, WILLIAM, & CO.)

TR: 7/17/1835; 8/21/1835

TREWORTHY, JOHN
w. Ellsworth, 1835. (See WILLIAM BENNETT & CO.; TREWORTHY & CHAMBERLAIN)

TUFTS, SAMUEL P.
w. Portland, 1797; painter and repairer of all kinds of chairs.

OT: 10/3/1797

VERY [Joseph] & HAGGET [John]
w. Portland, 1818; chairmakers; painters and repairers of old chairs.

PG: 9/1/1818

VERY, JOSEPH
w. Portland, 1813-1818; chairmaker, painter, and repairer of old chairs; originally of Grant & Very which dissolved July, 1813.

EA: 10/28/1813
PG: 9/1/1818

WARDELL, GEORGE J.
w. Hanover, 1850; age 24 in 1850; painter and cabinetmaker.

FC, 1850: Me., r. 262, p. 230

WATERMAN, HENRY P. & CO.
w. Bangor, 1827; painter and glazier; took over shop occupied by ISAAC R. PARK, 8/8/1827. (See PARK, ISAAC; WOOD, ORLANDO T.)

BR: 8/8/1827

WELLS [Moses] & HASKELL [William S.]
w. Augusta, 1842-1843; partnership between WELLS, cabinet/furniture maker, and HASKELL, gilder.

KJ: 12/2/1842; 3/30/1843

WHITE, DAVID, Jr.
w. Portland, 1850; age 23 in 1850; chair painter.

FC, 1850: Me., r. 252, p. 67.

WHITE, SAMUEL
w. Fairfield, Dexter, Exeter, 1830s - 1849; d. 1849; chairmaker and painter; chair dating from 1820s made in Fairfield, and chair dating from 1840s made

in Exeter have very similar decorating, suggesting same individual painted the two items.

Federal Census: 1850 (Maine), MSS, (at Maine State Archives), Vo. 27 (Exeter), Schedule 3, no. 19.

White, Almira L., *Genealogy of the Descendants of John White of Wenham and Lancaster, Mass., 1638-1900, 3 v., Haverhill, Mass: Charles Brothers, Printer, 1900, II, 203.*

WILLIAMS, JOHN

b. Chesterville, Maine, Jan. 6, 1801; w. Chesterville, 1827, Mount Vernon, 1827-1885; d. June 18, 1888; a cabinetmaker and possibly painter; son of Thomas Williams, a joiner.

FC, 1850: Me., r. 257, p. 374.
FIC, 1870: Me., Mt. Vernon.
KCRD: 59, 200; 62, 469; 63, 426.
KCRP: W8; File 12, Dochet 4982.
Lilly and Hewing, [Chesterville] Town Records, p. 21.
MBD, 1855, 1869, 1874-75, 1880, 1885.
Jackson, et al., *Maine 1830 Census List.*
Jackson, et al., *Maine 1840 Census List.*
Sewall, History of Chesterville, p. 17.

WOOD, ORLANDO T.

w. Bangor, 1828; age 44 in 1850; house, ship, and sign ornamental painter and glazier; shop formerly occupied by I.R. PARK and later by HENRY P. WATERMAN & CO. (See PARK, ISAAC; WATERMAN, HENRY P. & CO.)

FC, 1850: Me., r. 264, p. 66
BR: 4/22/1828

Index